GOLDEN RETRIEVERS
TODAY

VALERIE FOSS

New York

Maxwell Macmillan Canada
Toronto

Maxwell Macmillan International
New York Oxford Singapore Sydney

Howell Book House
Macmillan Publishing Company
866 Third Avenue
New York, NY 10022

Maxwell Macmillan Canada, Inc.
1200 Eglinton Avenue East
Suite 200
Don Mills, Ontario M3C 3N1

Printed in Singapore

Macmillan Publishing Company is part of the Maxwell Communication Group of Companies.

Library of Congress Cataloging-in-Publication Data

Foss, Valerie
        Golden retrievers today / Valerie Foss.
                p.   cm.
        ISBN 0-87605-184-0
        1. Golden retrievers.   I. Title.
SF429.G63F67 1994
636.7'52–dc20   93-38103
                                                                                CIP

Macmillan books are available at special discounts for bulk purchases for sales promotions, premiums, fund-raising, or educational use. For details, contact:

Special Sales Director
Macmillan Publishing Company
866 Third Avenue
New York, NY 10022

10 9 8 7 6 5 4 3 2 1

Contents

Acknowledgements

My thanks are due to Marcia Schlehr, Mercedes Hitchcock and Nona Bauer, whose help with the North American chapter was invaluable. A further 'thank you' to Marcia for her superb line drawings and to all the people who sent me photographs of their American dogs, especially Joan Luria, whose photos of some of the show 'greats' are lovely to have in the book.

I must also thank Daphne Philpott (Field Trials)and Joan Lavender (Obedience) for their help with the Training chapters. Treble thanks to Pat Busch (Germany) for her help with the chapter on Europe, for her lovely photographs of Guisachan House today, and for all the information relating to the link between Sir Edwin Landseer and Guisachan. Thanks to Henric Fryckstrand for all his help on Scandinavia, and Mike Ramsey for Australian information.

My thanks also to David Dalton, whose outstanding photographs illustrate so many pages, to the other photographers I have used, to *Dog World* for the sequence of trimming photos, and to all those who have lent me photographs. Thanks finally to Mavis Chapman for typing the manuscript – and to all those, not mentioned by name, who have helped me so much with this project.

VALERIE FOSS

Chapter One

HISTORY OF THE BREED

THE FIRST SPORTING DOGS

As early as the fourteenth century, Spaniels (bigger than the Spaniel breeds of today) were used for driving game and for hawking, and from these dogs Setters were evolved. By the beginning of the nineteenth century shooting men were beginning to train their Setters and Pointers to retrieve game, but it was not until 1830 onwards that sportsmen started to work on a breed to use specifically for retrieving. At this stage, the aim was to pass on working ability as well as particular individual characteristics, and the gundog breeds were mated among themselves.

Sportsmen were not content to have a good, working gundog, there was also an element of competition. The first trial for Setters and Pointers took place on April 18th 1865 on the Bedfordshire estate owned by Samuel Whitbread MP. The dogs were judged for nose, pace and range, temperament, plus style. In 1867 two meetings took place, one being the National Pointer and Setter and Retriever trials at Stafford.

It was by now becoming apparent that breeding regulations were required, and there were calls for a stud book and an administrative body to govern the breeding of pedigree dogs, in the same way that the Jockey Club governed the thoroughbred horse world. So, in April 1873 the Kennel Club was founded by S.E. Shirley of Ettington Park, near Stratford-upon-Avon. Its purpose was to provide a body designed to legislate on canine affairs. The first recognisable dog show was held at Newcastle-upon-Tyne on June 28th and 29th, 1859. One of the organisers was R.W. Pape, whose descendant, Miss Patricia Pape, shows Goldens Retrievers under the Abbotsford prefix. Other shows followed, and the sport of dog-showing became increasingly popular.

THE SHOOTING SCENE

In its traditional form, shooting was part of country life. The owner of a country house would walk his estate with his Setter and shoot about ten birds a day with his muzzle-loading gun. But by the 1880s the scene changed dramatically with the introduction of new weapons, which brought about a new scale of shooting, and a new social significance. The steel-barrelled, breach-loading shotgun came into being, with its single trigger. Better guns led to better shots, and the gamekeeper's job started to change. The priority was now to rear tame birds that could be driven to the guns by beaters. The far-reaching impact of these changes can be seen with the comparative figures of 39 birds shot on a Norfolk estate in 1821, and sixty years later 5,363 birds were killed. Lord de Grey, an excellent shot, calculated that between 1867 and 1923 he shot 250,000 pheasants, 150,000 grouse and 100,000 partridge.

The Prince of Wales, later King Edward VII, was a keen shot, and Sandringham soon became one of the finest shooting estates in the country. Famous for their pheasant shoots were Welbeck, Blenheim, Chatsworth and Holkham. In the north of England and on the Scottish moors, grouse abounded. The typical shooting party was made up of smart society transferred from the town to the country. Shooting was easier for middle-aged men with society pretensions to take up than hunting, and the whole sport became inseparable with wealth, status and fashion. It was a very expensive business to rear the birds, to employ the gamekeepers and the beaters, and the house parties themselves were run on a lavish scale.

At this time, the dogs resembled some of the modern breeds, but they were of a mixed or polyglot ancestry and were not well-defined varieties. Ability was all, and local strains as breeds were maintained and guarded. The new aim was to try to produce a breed for retrieving only, and that meant a dog with a good nose and a soft mouth, who was obedient, without the Setter's desire to range out. Sportsmen crossed their retrieving Setters with the smaller St Johns Newfoundland Dog. These dogs were brought into Britain by the Newfoundland fishing fleets and were unloaded in different ports. The well-documented early history of the Labrador Retriever records that in 1823 the 2nd Earl of Malmesbury imported the 'Little Newfoundler', later re-named the Labrador, from the Newfoundland fishing fleet which docked in Poole Harbour.

The woodcut illustration from Colonel Hutchinson's book shows the cross between Water Spaniel and Newfoundland Dog, between Water Spaniel and Setter Dog, between Setter and Newfoundland Dog. Depending on the cross, offspring could be black, liver, black-and-tan or brindled, with a height of about 24 inches. Yellow-coloured puppies from black parents were not unknown.

THE BREED'S PIONEER

The scene was now set, and all it needed was the inspiration and advanced thinking of Dudley Coutts Marjoribanks (pronounced Marshbanks) for the emergence of the Golden Retriever.

Dudley Marjoribanks (known as DCM) was born in 1820, the third son of Edward Marjoribanks, who was a partner in Coutts Bank (the Royal Bank). The Marjoribanks were an old Scottish family, and among their number were Lord Provosts and MPs. DCM's mother, Georgina de Lautour, was the daughter of a wealthy French merchant. According to a biography written by DCM's granddaughter recounting her mother's life, DCM was devoted to animals and to sport of every kind.

DCM's godmother was the widow of old Mr Coutts, and on his death she married the Duke of St Albans. DCM was her great favourite; she promised him a place in the bank, and hoped to marry him to Angela Burdett-Coutts, the granddaughter who inherited the Coutts' fortune. However, his godmother died when DCM was only seventeen, and neither of these plans for his advancement were realised. He did not become a suitor for the "richest woman in England's hand", and when he asked for his partnership in the bank, he was refused on the grounds that he was "totally unacquainted with business habits".

DCM was swift to fend for himself, and Sir Henry Meux offered him a directorship of the Meux Brewery. In 1848, after three months courtship, he married the lovely Isabel Hogg, daughter of Sir James Weir Hogg, Speaker in the House of Commons, MP for Honiton. In time, DCM became MP for Berwick-on-Tweed, and he took advantage of the long Parliamentary recess to devote his time to sporting pursuits in the Highlands of Scotland.

He rented shooting estates, and one of his favourites was Guisachan, belonging to William Fraser of Culbokie. A lovely story is told by the present owner's son, Donald Fraser, in his booklet on Guisachan. He relates that William Fraser of Culbokie gave a dinner party at Guisachan, and among the guests was Sir Dudley Marjoribanks. During the course of a sumptuous dinner, William Fraser said: "If anyone gave me £60,000 for Guisachan, I would sell it to-morrow. " From the other end of the table came DCM's prompt response: "Done!" Next morning Fraser approached DCM and said he had not meant it as a real offer – but DCM refused to release him, and so he acquired Guisachan. The accounts say that the Guisachan estate, then about 20,000 acres, was bought in 1854 for £52,000. In 1881 DCM was raised to the peerage, and took the title, Baron Tweedmouth – the 1st Lord Tweedmouth.

Always interested in all aspects of animal husbandry, Lord Tweedmouth had a prize-winning herd of Aberdeen Angus black-polled cattle. He also kept horses and ponies, and his precious dogs, which are described in the reminiscences of his daughter, Lady Aberdeen, as "Pointers celebrated for their prowess on the grouse moors, his favourite deer hounds, and the special yellow retrievers which he founded. In the house, Skye and Cairn Terriers". These special yellow retrievers were used for tracking and also for retrieving game. Due to the research of Elma Stonex and the 6th Earl of Ilchester, a great nephew of Lord Tweedmouth, we have his original stud book plus notes, which were kept from 1835 onwards rather like an inventory. His granddaughter, Lady Pentland, gave it to the Kennel Club, where it can still be seen today.

THE FIRST GOLDEN RETRIEVERS

The first yellow retriever was a single yellow from a litter of black wavy-coats, which Lord Tweedmouth bought from a Brighton cobbler who had got him from a keeper. The 1865 entry for Nous (the Gaelic name for wisdom) reads: "Lord Chichester's breed, pupped June 1864, purchased at Brighton." In this instance 'breed' means 'bred by', and this occurs many times ·throughout the book. I have a letter from the present Lord Hailsham (the longest-serving Lord Chancellor of this century), whose mother was married to Lord Tweedmouth's youngest son, the Hon Archie Marjoribanks, and this states: "My mother mentioned the Tweedmouth connection and that of Guisachan with the then new breed of Golden Retrievers, and, in particular, of a dog called Sol."

In those days all the dogs had names which referred to their colour, eg. Sol meaning sun, Crocus, Primrose etc. There was nothing odd in having a yellow puppy out of two blacks. Dr Bond Moore, who had a famous retriever kennel in the middle of the 1800s, is mentioned in Dalziel's *British Dogs* and Lee's *Modern Dogs* (late 1800s) as having a litter of Midnights, which included two fine pups of a pale-liver colour. There were many of these pups in otherwise all black litters, and the description 'liver' does not really describe the variations of the colour.

The next part of Lord Tweedmouth's plan involved a Tweed Water Spaniel, called Belle, given to him by a relative, David Robertson, MP for Ladykirk. In the stud book the bitch is entered in 1867 as "Ladykirk breed". We no longer have Tweed Water Spaniels, Norfolk Spaniels or English Water Spaniels, but in Richard Lawrence's book of 1816, *The Complete Farrier and British Sportsman* , he describes a water dog which sounds like a big Spaniel, used for wild fowling on the border coasts. The great canine author, Stonhenge, mentions the Tweedside Water Spaniel, which resembled a small English Retriever of a liver colour (authorities say the term 'liver' covered all the sandy colours from yellow to brown). Finally, there is evidence from the great authority on Retrievers, Stanley O'Neill. From 1899 to1906, O'Neill's father was superintendent of the Grimsby fish docks, and together they visited every port where fish was landed in England and Scotland. O'Neill says he saw hundreds of water dogs round Grimsby and Yarmouth, which were ships' dogs. It was well-known that curly-coats had originated with a cross from water dogs, with the aim of improving retrieving from water. In 1903 (he thought at Alnmouth), O'Neill saw

*Henry Edward, fifth
Earl of Ilchester,
pictured with Ada.*

*Zelstone (1880):
Great grandfather
of the last yellow
retrievers, Prim and
Rose, bred by Lord
Tweedmouth.*

men netting for salmon with a dog with a wavy or curly coat, which was tawny in colour. Airing his knowledge, he asked whether the dog was a water dog or a curly. The answer was a Tweed Water Spaniel from Berwick. In 1868 Nous and Belle were mated together. The resulting litter of four yellow puppies was the root foundation of Golden Retrievers as a distinct breed. The only dog, Crocus, was given to the Hon Edward Marjoribanks (2nd Lord Tweedmouth); Cowslip and Primrose were kept, and Ada was given to Lord Tweedmouth's nephew, the Earl of Ilchester. This bitch began the Ilchester strain (later prefix Melbury) in which black crosses were freely used. Much beloved by the Earl, Ada's gravestone can still be found on the Ilchester estate at Melbury. It is inscribed to "Ada – with the Golden Hair".

Breed: Yellow Retrievers
Sex: Bitches
Colour: Yellow
Bred by Owner:
1st Lord Tweedmouth
Guisachan, Beauly,
Inverness-shire.

PRIM and ROSE

The last two yellow retrievers recorded by Lord Tweedmouth.
Pedigree taken from particulars in Lord Tweedmouth's Stud Book
and extended where possible from Kennel Club Stud Book.
Colour only given where actually recorded by Lord Tweedmouth,
or for "Tracer" line from KC Stud Book

Date of Birth: 1889

NOUS (1884)
Yellow. One of four
yellow puppies.

  Jack (1875)
  Hon E. Marjoribanks
  2nd Lord Tweedmouth

    Sampson, red setter.
    Hon E. Marjoribanks
    2nd Lord Tweedmouth

    Cowslip (1868)
    Yellow. One of four
    yellow puppies

      Nous, yellow retriever,
      bought 1864, died
      1872

      Belle, Tweed water
      spaniel, given 1867
      from Ladykirk

  Zoe (1877)

    Sambo (Sir Henry
    Meux's presumed black
    flat or wavy coated
    retriever

    Topsy (1873)

      Tweed, Tweed water
      spaniel, given 1872
      from Ladykirk
      Cowslip (1868)

QUEENIE (1887)
Black. One of ten
black puppies.

  Tracer, black flat or
  wavy coated retriever,
  full brother to Ch.
  Moonstone

    Zelstone (1880),
    Black. Said to be half-
    bred Labrador

      Ben (1877)

      Bridget

    Think, black

      Dusk (1877)

      Ch. Wisdom (late
      Jenny), black, 1875

        Shot, half brother to Old Fag
        Bena, sister to Bess (Labrador)
        Thorn (late Bob), 1873,
        (**Victor**, 1869, x **Young Bounce**)
        Lady in Black
        (**Paris**, 1870, x **Lady Bonnie**)
        Moliere (1869)
        Maude,

        Nous, yellow retriever, 1864-1872
        Belle, Tweed water spaniel,

  Gill (1884)
  Yellow

    Jack (1875)

      Sampson, red setter.

      Cowslip (1868)

        Nous, yellow retriever, 1864- 1872
        Belle, Tweed water spaniel,

    Zoe (1877)

      Sambo (presumed
      black)

      Topsy (1873)

        Tweed, Tweed water spaniel
        Cowslip (1868)

It was found that a black dog and a yellow bitch invariably produced yellows, while some of each colour came from a yellow dog and a black bitch. From Lord Tweedmouth's stud book it is clear how thoughtfully the matings were planned from 1868, the date of the first litter, to 1890 when the book ends. Cowslip was mated to Tweed (a Tweed Water Spaniel), and four years later one of their puppies, Topsy, was put to a black retriever, called Sambo. From this mating a bitch called Zoe was kept, and in 1884 she was mated to her grand-dam's (Cowslip's) son, Jack, who was sired by Sampson out of an Irish Setter. Two of their puppies were Nous (N2) and Gill, whose pedigree showed Cowslip and Tweed appearing three times in four generations. In 1887 an outcross, Gill, was mated to Tracer, a full brother to the famous black wavy-coated Ch. Moonstone

– the result was ten black puppies! One of these blacks, Queenie, was mated to her dam's litter brother, the second Nous. Their two yellow puppies, Prim and Rose born 1889, were the last recorded by Lord Tweedmouth, who died in 1894.

In another line, Zoe had several litters by Sweep (black), who was recorded as bred by Lord Ilchester, and a descendant of Ada. At some time during the 1890s a sandy-coloured bloodhound was used as a cross. The descendants of this cross were dark-coloured, very big, powerful and ugly, and some were inclined to be savage.

THE VICTORIAN SHOOTING SCENE

It is often difficult to understand how early Goldens went to different parts of the country. A fact often forgotten is that Lord Tweedmouth mixed in the highest Victorian circles. Those circles had a very fixed routine. In her memoirs, Princess Alice, Duchess of Gloucester writes: "My childhood memories are dominated by houses because every year on a fixed rota we used to visit different ones at different seasons". One visit would be for the shooting season. Christopher Sykes' fascinating *Country House Camera* is filled with photographs taken by noble, keen, photographers. In the section 1870-1889 it describes the the pattern of life enjoyed by a house party in a large country house, especially a shooting party. The following excerpt is from this book:

"When breakfast was over the ladies retired, either to their rooms, all of which would have been furnished with a writing desk, or to the morning room, to read, embroider or write their letters and diaries. For the men there was invariably some kind of sporting activity, of which by far the most popular was shooting. It was a great distinction for a host to lay on a good shoot and to be a good shot, particularly since the Prince of Wales's passion for the sport had made it so fashionable. Men like Lord de Grey, Lord Ripon and Lord Walsingham, the finest shots of their day, set a new standard in the organisation of their shoots and the entertaining that went with them. There can be few country house albums that do not bear witness to the Prince of Wales's endless sporting tours. Wherever he went, a photographer would be on hand to record the triumphant party, their game laid out beside them, either in front of the house or in the field.

Guisachan House, pictured in the 1900s. Golden Retrievers are pictured on the left, Setters on the right.

"Of all the great shooting hosts, perhaps the strangest was the Duke of Westminster. In spite of the fact that he was the owner of one of the finest shoots in the country, he never specifically asked people to stay to shoot. Those lucky enough to know the form, however, never failed to arrive with the full paraphernalia of pheasant shooting included in their luggage. Lord Ernest Hamilton recalled how, on the advice of a friend, he dutifully arrived on his first visit to Eaton with his guns, but that there was not a whisper on that first night of any shooting the next day.

"This appeared to make little difference to most of the male guests who appeared at breakfast fully dressed in knickerbockers and shooting boots. There was still not a word from the Duke about shooting, and after a while the party dispersed in some despondency of mind to follow other pursuits. 'About half-past ten', he wrote, 'I was dejectedly smoking a cigarette in the hall, having by that time definitely abandoned all hope of shooting, when the Duke strolled dreamily up to me and said "Brought a gun?". I replied brightly that I had. "Care to come out and see if we can pick up a pheasant or two?" he continued.' The result of this somewhat nonchalant invitation was the slaughter of a thousand pheasants in the two hours before lunch. 'The Duke never shot after lunch,' continued Lord Ernest, 'but while he was shooting he liked to be busy.'

"The ladies joined the party for luncheon which took place either back at the house, or in some grandiose, medieval-style tent, and they might stay out to watch one or two drives in the afternoon."

THE BREED SPREADS

Among the photographs in *Country House Camera* is a picture of a group of keepers at Fenton, Northumberland, taken by Beatrice Countess of Durham. The dog at the end of the line-up is a definite Golden Retriever, and by this time Lord Tweedmouth had started his breeding plans. Could there be any connection? The 4th Earl of Durham's younger brother had changed his name to Meux (Sir Hedworth Meux), probably in order to inherit money or land. Recalling the pedigree of Prim and Rose, one of the dogs recorded is Sambo – Sir Henry Meux's flat or wavy-coated retriever. Sir Henry was a family friend and business colleague of Lord Tweedmouth. Sambo and Topsy produced Zoe, born 1877. Was this Zoe's brother or sister in the photograph?

Lord Tweedmouth had six children. His elder daughter, Mary, married Sir Matthew White Ridley, 1st Viscount Ridley of Blyth, Northumberland. The Ridley family were famous for their Setters, and I am sure some of Lord Tweedmouth's yellow retrievers went with his daughter to her new home. Lord Tweedmouth's son and heir, Edward, 2nd Lord Tweedmouth, married Lady Fanny Spencer Churchill, daughter of John, 7th Duke of Marlborough. Her mother, Frances, was the daughter of the Marquis of Londonderry. It was because the Tweedmouths sent their son to Harrow, not Eton, that his cousin, Winston Churchill, also went there. This led, indirectly, to more great families seeing the yellow retrievers at work.

Lord Tweedmouth's second daughter, Ishbel, made a great match and married the Earl of Aberdeen. A great liberal peer, he became Lord Lieutenant of Ireland and then Governor General of Canada. Ishbel was a great fighter for the poor and also for women's rights. Lord Tweedmouth's next son, Stewart, died as a youngster, and the two younger sons, Coutts and Archie, both went to America. Archie married Elizabeth, daughter of Judge Trimble Brown of Nashville. Archie died in January 1900, leaving a son Edward and a daughter Isabel. Edward had a brilliant career as an author and as an MP. He was heir presumptive to his cousin, the 3rd Lord Tweedmouth, who had no sons to succeed him. Sadly, Edward committed suicide on April 2nd 1932, and so on his cousin's death, the title became extinct.

The 1st Lord Tweedmouth came from a large family. His sister, the Hon Mrs Fox-Strangeways,

Sandy, bred by the fifth Earl of Ilchester, owned by Colonel le Poer Trench.

Sam, owned by Walter Earl of Dalkeith, bred by the Earl of Ilchester, pictured in 1886.

was the mother of the 5th Earl of Ilchester, and his son, the 6th Earl, married the daughter of the Marquess of Londonderry. The Marquess' wife was the sister of the 20th Earl of Shrewsbury, whose Ingestre Golden Retrievers are so important in the breed's early history. So it is easy to see, with all the connections, family and otherwise, how the 'yellow retrievers' spread.

THE RUSSIAN LEGEND

For many years there was a legend about the origin of the Golden Retriever, and it was widely believed that the breed was founded from a troupe of Russian circus dogs, purchased by the 1st Lord Tweedmouth and taken to Guisachan. The two greatest proponents of this theory were Colonel Hon le Poer Trench (St Huberts) and Mrs Charlsworth (Noranby). They did not have any proof, but as both were strong-minded, dictatorial characters, the theory took root.

It was not until 1952 that the theory was discredited, due to the findings of breed historian Elma Stonex and the 6th Earl of Ilchester, who used Lord Tweedmouth's stud book to substantiate their claims for the true origin of the breed. In 1960 the English Kennel Club officially recognised the origin of the breed as investigated by Elma Stonex and the Earl of Ilchester. A year earlier, due to the work of Rachel Elliott, the American Golden Retriever Club and the American Kennel Club officially recognised the origin.

The Russian Retriever: St Huberts Peter, painted by Maud Earl , presented to King George V.

In 1883 Colonel le Poer Trench had obtained a descendant of the original dogs from the Earl of Ilchester. This dog was called Sandy, and the Colonel decided to breed with him and keep his strain pure from the bloodhound cross – conveniently forgetting that the Ilchester breed had been crossed with black Labradors and wavy-coats from the beginning. The Colonel obtained a dog, called St Huberts Rock, from a ghillie in Scotland. His next plan was to get a bitch of 'pure' lines. This was difficult, but he met a Major who said he had a bitch, and who agreed to part with her to the Colonel. She was called St Huberts May (she was an albino). There was a delay of a couple of years, and then she was mated to Rock. She produced, in all, twenty-seven puppies.

The Colonel went off to Russia to try and get more of the 'original' strain, but failed. The Colonel then caused complications by inferring that the 1st Lord Tweedmouth had known about the St Hubert's dogs and his breeding programme. Seventeen years after the 1st Lord Tweedmouth's death, the Colonel registered at the Kennel Club the Marjoribanks and Ilchester breed of 'Yellow Russian Retrievers and Trackers', which the Kennel Club accepted as a separate breed. Crufts gave them classes in 1913, 1914, and 1915, and there is the Maud Earl painting of St Huberts Peter, who was given to King George V.

However, when the Colonel died, his will directed that all his dogs should be put down. Mrs Charlsworth carried on the story, stating that old gamekeepers from Guisachan said they remembered the Russian dogs arriving! But the concrete proof is contained in Lord Tweedmouth's stud book, which has no mention of Russian dogs whatsoever. The story of six or eight Russian circus dogs arriving in 1858 could not be true, for not only were there never more than four Retrievers recorded in the stud book up to 1866, but no kind of foreign breed or importation was ever mentioned. If this had been the case, it would have been an outstanding entry.

The 3rd Lord Tweedmouth told the Kennel Club that his grandfather had informed him that his first yellow retriever had been a single yellow from a litter of black wavy-coats. It was the 3rd Lord Tweedmouth who approved of the name Marjoribanks in the Colonel's registration of the title, but of nothing else. Maybe, if the Earl of Chichester, who bred the first Nous, had fought in the Crimean war (1853-1856) he might have brought back an ancestor of Nous, for we do know that breeds similar to Golden Retrievers existed in Europe and Russia.

There is one dog mentioned in the stud book, called Sancho, April 1868. No breeding is given, and he was clearly a failure as he is never mentioned again and had no place in the breeding programme. Sancho could be a circus name, and this would account for the keeper's story that a Russian dog did once appear. They spoke of the arrival of Nous in 1868, but he was already there. Perhaps Sancho was the dog they spoke of? However, no matter where this dog came from, he did not contribute to the breed.

THE TWEEDMOUTH LEGACY

When the 1st Lord Tweedmouth died, Guisachan passed to the 2nd Lord Tweedmouth. He kept no records from 1894 to 1905. As a young man, he had Crocus from the first litter and owned the Irish Setters, Samson and Jack, used in his father's breeding programmes. His name is in Volume I of the Kennel Club Stud book as the owner of Sultan, a liver-coloured retriever dog, whelped 1867, by Moscow, a liver retriever out of a Tweedside Spaniel. The 2nd Lord Tweedmouth was an important Liberal politician and held high offices of state: First Lord of the Admiralty, MP for Berwick, Parliamentary Secretary to the Treasury and Chief Liberal Whip (1892-1894), Lord Privy Seal and Chancellor of the Duchy of Lancaster. But by 1905 he was in serious financial and personal trouble. His beloved wife, Fanny, had died of cancer in 1904. He sold old masters worth £48,895, and Brook House in London, and finally, Guisachan itself was sold in 1908. It was bought by Lord Portsmouth, who for the next twenty-seven years used it for shooting or rented it out. Some of the dogs went with the house.

In a letter from the then Earl of Portsmouth to Rachel Elliott of the USA in 1965, he writes that his uncle, the Earl of Portsmouth, at that time bought the house with all the Golden Retrievers there. When in 1909 the then Earl went as a little boy to live with his aunt and uncle at Hurstbourne in Hampshire, one of his first memories was meeting the yellow dogs there. They had been brought down from Guisachan to use as shooting dogs. They were kept by the head keeper, and two lived in the house. That summer, the small boy went to Guisachan for the first time, and found the dogs were not only used for retrieving but also for tracking wounded deer. Guisachan was sold by the family in 1932, and the two best bitches with a litter of puppies were brought to Hampshire. Later on the line was carried on by using Mrs Charlsworth's Noranby dogs.

Guisachan's fortunes were now on the wane, and the end for the mansion house came in 1939 when Lady Islington bought it for £1,500 and started to strip it for demolition. Now all that is left is a picturesque shell. The estate, at last, has returned to the Frasers. In 1966 it went to Colonel James Fraser MC, a direct descendant of the Frasers of Leckmelm and Balnain, and it is now in the hands of his younger son, Donald. In fact, Guisachan 'The Place of the Fir' is still visited by many people today, as it is in the vicinity of Loch Ness country, and visitors stay at Tomich House, a former shooting lodge

After twelve months of nervous illness, the 2nd Lord Tweedmouth died in September 1909. He

Guisachan House as it is today, now owned by Donald Fraser.

was succeeded by his son, Dudley Churchill Marjoribanks, a Lord in Waiting to King George V. He married the daughter of the Earl of Middleton, but they had no sons – only two daughters. As his cousin, Edward Marjoribanks, died before him, the title became extinct.

Although no records were kept after 1890, a few Guisachan names at the turn of the century have come through to us as parents of important registered dogs. They are Rock, Conon, Lucifer, Amber, Lute, Brass, Glen, Cruna and Haddo. The most important information is that Viscount Harcourt got the foundation of his breed from two puppies acquired from the Guisachan keeper, John MacLennan. The mother of the puppies was out of a bitch called Lady belonging to the Hon Archie Marjoribanks – pure Guisachan breeding.

PICTORIAL EVIDENCE

It is quite remarkable we have so many photographs of the early dogs. Nous, himself, is pictured at Guisachan – once with the keepers and dogs, and once with the keeper, Simon Munro. The Guisachan stalker, Simon Fraser, is photographed with Comet, Conan and Ginger in 1903. There is a photo of Colonel the Hon W. le Poer Trench's group of St Huberts, taken in 1906. Crocus is pictured with Lady Fanny Marjoribanks, and there are many of Lord Harcourt's Culhams. The Earl of Ilchester's Ada and Robin are in photographs, and the Hon Archie Marjoribank's Lady is pictured in America and Canada.

The early Golden Retriever is also well served in paintings. There are quite a few paintings of dogs that look like Golden Retrievers, well before Lord Tweedmouth's time. It is known from the Marchioness of Aberdeen's Memoirs (the 1st Lord Tweedmouth's daughter) that the famous animal painter Sir Edwin Landseer, stayed at Guisachan and taught Lady Aberdeen painting. Many of the Landseer paintings had early retrievers in them – had he seen them at Guisachan? Landseer was a keen sportsman; shooting and deer stalking were amongst his favourite hobbies.

His close friend was the portrait painter, Sir Francis Grant. Sir Francis painted a shooting party at Ranton Abbey in 1840 (it hangs in Shugborough, home of the Earl of Litchfield). It is a very large painting, and on the right-hand side, amongst some Spaniels, is a Retriever with a pheasant, looking very like a golden of today. Gourlay Steele, the Queen's animal painter in Scotland, painted a large picture of Lord Tweedmouth's famous Aberdeen Angus herd in 1890. It hangs in the Royal Highland Society rooms at Edinburgh. In the left-hand corner are two Golden Retrievers looking at the herd. One dog is standing, the other lying down. Steele also painted another large oil painting that used to hang in the dining room at Guisachan, showing the Hon Mary Majoribanks on Sunflower, with Cowslip or Primrose from the first litter of yellow retrievers, born in 1868.

In 1875 the Hon H. Graves painted the portrait of Henry Edward 5th Earl of Ilchester with Ada, who looks to be very much of modern size. There is also a painting by L.G. Goddard depicting Ada and a horse, dated 1873. Maud Earl painted St Huberts Peter, which can now be obtained as a print. In 1906 Maud Earl painted an Ilchester retriever, Czar, and Prince and Peter from the St Huberts were painted by Wright Barker. There is also a lovely painting of Sandy, the original dog owned by le Poer Trench, bred by the Earl of Ilchester, and another of Walter, owned by the Earl of Dalkeith. Not to be forgotten, are the watercolours by R. Ward Binks, showing Mrs Cottingham's famous Woolley champions. So, if you have your Golden Retriever painted or photographed today, remember, you are carrying on a great tradition.

Ch. Cracksavon Charmed I'm Sure of Suregold.   *David Dalton*

Chapter Two

CHOOSING YOUR GOLDEN RETRIEVER

WHY A GOLDEN RETRIEVER?

Once you have given your heart to a Golden Retriever, no other breed will suit. Intelligent, kind, loving and sensible, this breed combines all the virtues with glamorous good looks. Golden Retrievers can still do the work they were originally bred for, making clever, enthusiastic gundogs. They can work well in Obedience and Agility competitions, they are successful as guide dogs for the blind, and they also work well as therapy dogs, visiting the sick and the elderly. The great beauty of the Golden Retriever is that they carry out these tasks with such kindness. They learn with you, and never try to make the owner feel they are not really in control. The Golden Retriever is not a difficult dog to keep in terms of size and coat care, and they house train quite easily.

These are all the plus points of owning the breed. However, you and your family must be aware of what is involved in taking on a puppy. Do not be misled by seeing beautiful photographs of endearing puppies, or by a brief meeting with someone who owns a Golden Retriever – the reality of caring for a lively, mischievous puppy may be quite different! Puppies need a lot of attention. Goldens, as medium-sized dogs, are not cheap to feed if it is to be done properly. Veterinary attention if needed, is costly. Insurance cover for veterinary fees is an excellent idea, but it is not a maintenance contract to cover vaccination, boosters, worming treatments etc.; it is a safeguard against unexpected veterinary bills.

While a puppy is growing up, it is almost inevitable that possessions in the home will be damaged through chewing. For the most part, this is the fault of the owner for leaving chewable objects within reach – but we are all prone to carelessness. Golden Retrievers should not be kennelled as single dogs, and to go out and leave a dog in a garage all day is cruel. You must, therefore, have a lifestyle that will accommodate the needs of your dog. This also applies to the need to give your Golden Retriever regular exercise – come rain or shine. It is also worth considering that if you are not going to take your Golden on holiday with you, there is the expense of boarding kennels to add to the holiday budget.

These are the drawbacks of dog ownership, and they are applicable to the vast majority of breeds. However, once you have fallen under the spell of the Golden Retriever's charms, it is unlikely that you will want another breed of dog. Often people buy their first Golden Retriever because they know a friend who owns one, or they have seen a picture in a paper or book. In fact, this was how I got my first Golden Retriever. Our dog, a Scottie, had died at the age of fifteen and it was awful without a dog. I was determined to do this choosing correctly, and so I got a book from the library, and read all the descriptions of the different breeds and looked at the photographs. They were of famous dogs of that era and I fell in love with two pictures, one of the Golden

The biddable nature of the Golden Retriever makes it ideal for training as a guide dog for the blind.

Guide Dogs for the Blind Association.

Retriever bitch, Ch. Stubbings Golden Gloria, and the other was of the lovely Gordon Setter bitch, Ch. Painters Nancy.

The next step was to find some puppies of the two breeds. In our local paper there was a litter of Golden Retrievers advertised. That was it! Off we set to see the litter and I found Kim, who was the start of a love affair with a breed which has brought so much into my life. I did not buy a Gordon Setter, although I award Challenge Certificates in the breed, and I have judged them all over the world. I also kept some part of the Setter theme because I married a man with English Setters, and over the years I have owned and loved many famous Setters. They fit in beautifully with Goldens.

At a show I had entered English Setters, plus 'Clem', one of my Golden Retrievers. We stood between the two rings, Clem observing the English Setters with a knowing eye as they went past. My friend looked down at her and said: "I bet every morning she wakes up, looks at her legs and thinks, "Oh dear, the spots haven't come yet!"

THE PROCESS OF SELECTION

The subject of choosing a puppy is usually discussed in two separate parts, depending on whether you are looking for a pet or for a show puppy, with the assumption that the two can never be found in the same litter. This is a potential danger in a breed that is as popular as the Golden Retriever, as there are those with more mercenary motives who are anxious to supply to pet homes, without finding out if the purchaser has a suitable lifestyle to accommodate a dog, let alone a Golden Retriever. However, when a litter is bred by a caring breeder/exhibitor, there is the right puppy for both pet and show homes.

If you are buying a show puppy, you will probably have a certain amount of knowledge about the breed, and you will know what you are looking for. It may be that you already have a show dog, or perhaps your Golden Retriever's showing days are nearing a close and you wish to start again with the knowledge you have gained. However, if you are choosing a show puppy or a pet, it is important to spend time choosing your puppy. Do not be pushed into buying a puppy you have doubts about. Remember, the responsibility you are taking on should last for the next ten to fifteen years.

CHOOSING A PET PUPPY

FINDING A BREEDER

Do not go to a kennel that sells lots of breeds. It is much better to go to a specialist breeder, where you can be confident of buying a healthy, well-reared puppy. What makes reputable breeders? They will only breed from eye-tested and hip-scored stock. They are as keen to find out if you are suitable to have one of their puppies, as you are keen to find out if their puppies are suitable for you!

Where do you find a reputable breeder? Your national Kennel Club will be able to put you in touch with a breed club in your area, and the secretary will have list of breeders. The secretary may even know which breeders have puppies available.

When you visit the breeder you will, hopefully, find well-reared, well-fed puppies, and, importantly, a well-cared-for dam. When you go to visit a litter, always ask to see the dam, and have a good look at the condition of the kennels, or wherever the puppies are kept. Puppies should be reared in a clean, pleasant-smelling environment.

MALE OR FEMALE

You will probably have decided whether you want a dog or a bitch before you go to view a litter. In Goldens, the dogs are just as loving as the bitches. The advantages of owning a bitch is that they are smaller than the male; a bitch is not likely to roam or stray, and will be easier to house train.

The disadvantages are that a bitch will come in season twice a year, and at this time she must not be allowed to go out off the lead. The in-season bitch can be very messy with loss of blood. If you have already got a dog (male), you must be able to make separate housing arrangements when the bitch comes in season. Pedigree bitch puppies sometimes cost more than the males, and often more bitches are booked from the litter, and so they may not be as easy to obtain.

ASSESSING THE PUPPIES

Be honest with the breeder about your requirements dog-wise. You will probably be shown only the puppies that are available for sale. The breeder may well have reserved a puppy from the litter as a potential show prospect or breeding prospect. In fact, it is often only minor points that.

Good rearing is obvious when you see a litter of well-fed, clean, bright-eyed puppies.

R. Dixon.

separate the puppies in this sort of litter. Essentially, you are looking for temperament and health. Look for the friendly, bold, playful puppy who is nicely-rounded, not too fat nor too thin, and definitely no 'pot belly', as this usually indicates worms. Eyes and ears should be clean; there should be no scabs or skin lesions, and there should be a nice feel to the coat at this stage, which is still at the fluffy stage. The puppy should be straight in bone, and you should check that the jaws are correct. The way the teeth fit in baby puppies' mouths is difficult to describe because each line or strain can be different at seven to eight weeks. However, at this age, the front top teeth should overlap the bottom teeth. In respect of colour, Golden Retrievers usually finish several shades darker than the colour of the puppy coat.

COLLECTING YOUR PUPPY

You will be able to collect your puppy between eight and ten weeks, but you can prepare by getting a copy of the breeder's diet sheet so you will be able to get the same food in as the puppy has been fed on. Never change a puppy's diet straightaway, as that is asking for stomach upsets.

When you go to pick up your puppy, the breeder should also give you some important documents. These include a puppy registration certificate, which you will need to send off to the Kennel Club in order to transfer ownership. You will be given the pedigree of the puppy, which is a form containing the names of sire and dam, and going back three, four, or five generations. In the UK some breeders insure their puppies to cover the first few weeks in a new home. The owner then has the option to continue the policy or not.

CHOOSING A SHOW PUPPY

FIRST ESSENTIALS

Choosing a puppy for show has many points that are similar to choosing a pet puppy, and in two points they are exactly the same. You are looking for a fearless pup with a loving disposition, who is obviously in tip-top health and condition. You will have told the breeder you want to show, and, hopefully, to get to the top and then found a dynasty of your own. Eye and hip certificates are, again, essential for the sire and dam.

MALE OR FEMALE

In this instance, the bitch is usually chosen because of her breeding potential. Your male, however outstanding, is unlikely to get many bookings at stud. Experienced breeders are unlikely to use the services of a novice stud dog, supervised by a novice stud dog owner.

FINDING A BREEDER

Nobody can guarantee that your puppy will grow up to be a winner, but people who have bred a strain for many years can often tell how their strain will develop. You will also be able to see the kennels' adults, and so you will have some idea as to how your puppy will develop. Many books recommend that you go to shows and sit and watch and then decide which lines you like the best and get in touch with those breeders. I feel that this system can leave you in a very muddled state. What you want is a breeder who has sold many winners to other people, especially to novices.

ASSESSING THE PUPPIES

The breeder of a litter always has an advantage over the buyer who sees the puppies for a very short time. For the breeder, it pays to spend time just sitting and watching them. You want balance in your puppy, with everything in proportion. Good shoulders are essential, with a well-laid back and correct angulation of the upper arm. You are looking for a good reach of neck, strong, rounded bone, straight, strong front legs and not too loose on elbows. The hindquarters should have a good turn of stifle. Tail carriage is always difficult as baby puppies will, in play and in feeding, bring their tails up. However, you can look to see if the tail flows on nicely from the topline.

In puppies, the head will vary, depending on what line the puppy comes from. It is best to look for the happy medium, i.e. a skull that is not coarse or thick, a broad deep muzzle, a good stop (that is the indentation between the eyes), and ears set not too high nor too low. Do not worry if the ears look large – puppies ears soon balance out. You want the teeth to grow into a perfect scissor bite. The 'norm' seems to be for the front top teeth to really come over the bottom teeth. The eyes should not be too round nor bulging, nor too small – all these will give the wrong expression. At this stage they will be blue-grey in colour, and this gradually changes to dark-brown over the next weeks. Pigmentation on the nose, eye rims and lips should be black.

I find that the best time to catch what the puppy will grow into is between six and seven weeks, although I know of one very famous breeder who picks her show prospects when just born and they are still wet. However, I find that after seven weeks the balanced stage goes and the puppies are in the gawky stage. You look at your young star and think this has all been a big mistake. But if you want to show your puppy, be patient – and gradually the parts balance out again. It is not the basic construction that changes radically; it is usually the appendages that can look unbalanced, such as the ears and the tail. Remember, the colour of a puppy is usually lighter than its colour as an adult. In fact, the ears will show the colour the puppy will probably be when mature.

The socialisation and handling of baby puppies is very important. The dam teaches the puppies much of their behaviour, and as they play they learn what is allowed and what is not allowed. However, they must also learn to be handled by humans. Great care has to be taken for fear of introducing infection among the unvaccinated litter, but the advantage of the caring breeder is again shown in this aspect. The breeder will check that anyone who handles the puppies is not

A puppy with show potential, appearing well-balanced with everything in proportion.

wearing clothes or shoes that have been in contact with other dogs, and only short sessions of play will be allowed

It is a great advantage for puppy-picking, if, from four weeks old, the puppies are used to standing still for one minute on a safe surface (a small piece of fleecy rug with velcro on the back so it does not slip, is ideal). A final point about picking a puppy for show is that you must bear in mind that it does not finish with the picking. The conditioning, feeding and exercise are vital in producing the final show puppy. I have often seen two puppies of comparable merit, one kept by the experienced breeder/exhibitor, the other kept by the novice who does not heed all the advice given, and by the time the two dogs are ready to be shown, they look like different breeds! When you first start to show your puppy it is the culmination of a conditioning cycle that started when your puppy first came home with you.

CHOOSING A WORKING RETRIEVER
If you want your Golden Retriever as a pet, but also to work in the field and possibly to run in Field Trials, contact a breeder of Field Trial Golden Retrievers. All Golden Retrievers will have some working instinct, but if you want to do a particular discipline with your dog, you need to go to the breeder who has bred for generations for biddability, style and speed; for these are very much inherited factors.

Yes, of course, people have bought from kennels with dogs on a five-generation pedigree that produced no field workers, and due to luck, chance, the owner's skill at training – call it what you will – they have turned the dog into a reasonable trial dog. However, that is doing things in a very

Jacko Of Norwich: If you want a working dog you should go to a kennel that specialises in working stock.

David Dalton.

roundabout fashion. If your hobby is climbing you need the correct equipment. You can climb without the equipment, but your chances of success are dramatically lessened.

CHOOSING AN OLDER DOG
You may decide that you will be better suited with an older dog, and again, we will take this from the two angles, pet or show.

THE COMPANION DOG
The advantage of an adult is that you will miss out on the house-training and chewing stages of puppyhood. The adult may have received some training, but not necessarily, and the older dog will certainly have got used to the ways of other people. If you go to one of the breed club rescue services, they will probably know why the dog needs rehoming. The dog is vetted, you are also vetted for suitability, and you usually have the dog on a trial period.

Sometimes, a breeder will have an adult available for rehoming because a problem has arisen in the original home. It may be that the owner has become ill and is unable to give exercise, a marriage break-up may have caused a change in circumstance, or the original owner may have died. Find out as much as possible about the dog, and always insist on a trial period of around two weeks, which is best for the dog, and for you.

THE SHOW DOG
If you acquire an adult as a show dog, you will, of course, pay more. By the age of six months you

If you decide to acquire an adult, whether for a companion or for show, you must give the dog a chance to adapt to its new home.

Steve Nash.

can see much more of the finished article, and less can go wrong with the early conditioning and training, which has been done for you. From the age of twelve months, eyes and hips will have been certificated, so again, the price goes up. If you are lucky you may come across a breeder who has run on two puppies – not being able to decide which one to keep at the puppy stage – but by six months one must go. Sometimes a breeder has to cut down on numbers, and stock that is normally not for sale will come on the market. If you feel an adult is a good way to start breeding and exhibiting, do not rush into acquiring a dog. Visit the shows, visit the breeders in your area, wait, keep your ear to the ground, and your luck might be in!

Chapter Three

CARING FOR YOUR GOLDEN RETRIEVER

FEEDING

We live in an age in which people are much more aware of the importance of a well-balanced diet for themselves, and this attitude tends to enter into their feelings of how they should feed their dog. You want to maintain your Golden Retriever's fitness and health, and when you first go into the pet store to buy your dog's food you can be surrounded by so many different brands and varieties that the choice becomes very difficult.

There are some nutritional myths which seem to have been passed down. Firstly, the belief dogs get bored eating the same food day after day. Dogs do not need to taste different flavours to enjoy their food. Actually, it can do more harm than good, and it can cause diarrhoea. That is why when you buy a puppy or an adult, you should, initially, keep to the same diet which has been fed previously. If you want to change the diet, do it gradually, putting some of the new food with the old food and gradually changing over. This should be done over a five to ten day period until the new food has completely replaced the old diet. Dogs who are finicky eaters can often be made that way by their owners, who keep on chopping and changing their dog's food.

The dog of today has the same digestive tract as the wild dog. The tract is short and the process simple. Food passes through quickly, and thus the dog must have very digestible food. Food is eaten quickly; it is often bolted. Dogs do not chew or grind the food down in the mouth. The dog has a very short small intestine (4m), and this cannot cope with large volumes of food. The food has only a short time to undergo digestion. However, the dog has quite a large stomach, which can stretch and predisposes the dog to gastric dilation and torsion, i.e. bloat.

NUTRITIONAL COMPONENTS
Food is made up of carbohydrates, fats, proteins, minerals and vitamins.

CARBOHYDRATES: These provide the bulk of energy for daily activity. Such energy is measured in calories. Roughly, larger animals need 49 calories per kg (21 per lb). As well as providing energy, carbohydrates are essential in that they supply the bulk needed to satisfy hunger pangs, and to keep the bowels with normal faecal consistency.

FATS: These are necessary to the canine diet for the calories they provide and they help to govern texture of the food. Deficiency of fats can cause dry, scaly skin and can affect the resistance to disease.

PROTEINS: Digestion breaks proteins down into amino acids and they are then absorbed and used for normal growth and daily body metabolism. If certain essential amino acids are not in the diet, symptoms of deficiency will appear. An interesting point is that not only is the amount of protein offered important, but also its quality is important.

MINERALS AND VITAMINS: Dogs require small, but essential amounts of minerals and vitamins to regulate the body's activities. As with human feeding, your Golden Retriever needs a balanced diet with the right amount of protein, fat, carbohydrate, vitamins and minerals to maintain top-class condition.

FEEDING METHODS
There are many different methods of feeding your dog, and there is a tremendous variety of foods. Remember, your dog relies on you to understand its needs and to feed an appropriate diet. Let us examine the different methods of feeding dogs, remembering they are carnivores, which means they have a preference for food of animal origin. In the wild they would also eat the stomach containing vegetable matter as well. Feeding only meat would be an unbalanced diet, for roughage is essential.

COMPLETE
Complete foods are what the label says – 'complete', i.e. they have the correct balance of protein, animal and vegetable fats (saturated and unsaturated) carbohydrates, fibre, minerals and vitamins. The balance is adjusted to suit the individual dog's needs for growth, reproduction, maintenance and activity, as long as you follow the instructions at to amounts, and the type needed for your dog's life.

The complete foods tend to all look different: flaked ingredients, pelleted ingredients, and some are a mixture of both flakes and pellets. Most of them can be fed soaked or dry. There are several advantages to complete feeding. You do not have to give extra additives, you do not need to add any extra food, and it is easy to prepare. Your dog should have clean bowls for food and water. I find the stainless steel bowls, obtainable from pet stores, are the best. They wash up so well and last for many years. You should always leave a bowl of clean water down at all times., but this is especially important with complete diets. Dogs fed on complete diets tend to excrete a larger amount of faeces than dogs fed on meat and biscuits, and as they drink a lot of water they tend to produce more urine.

There are diet ranges that contain no artificial colouring, flavouring and preservatives, and there has been quite a lot of scaremongering over ethoxyquin and other preservatives. You can buy vegetarian diets, and if your dog gets too fat, there are weight-loss diets available. You must choose the right food for the job and fitness scheme your dog will follow. For example, the high-protein puppy food is not designed for the veteran. Working dogs, such as sheep dogs, police dogs and guide dogs for the blind, need more energy than a house dog.

The feeding of puppies is especially important as an animal fed incorrectly during puppyhood may suffer the effects of malnutrition for the rest of their life. The feeding of old dogs is also different, and often your vet will recommend a specialised diet. Little and often is a good rule with elderly dogs.

TRADITIONAL
Another method of feeding is that of providing meat, fresh and then cooked (unless fit for human

consumption and able to be fed raw), canned or dried, plus a good-quality biscuit meal. To get the balance right you will need to supplement with the right minerals and vitamins. The biscuit meal is soaked, and when it has absorbed the liquid it is twice its size, soft and ready to be mixed with the meat. Sometimes, with very good feeders, it is better to feed the meat on its own and give the biscuit ration in the shape of large, flat biscuits or biscuits shaped like bones etc.

NATURAL ADDITIVES
Many people feed natural cure herbal tablets or powder, and I find seaweed is good for encouraging coat texture and growth. I use raspberry leaf as a whelping aid, and many people I know swear by oil of primrose as a general coat conditioner.

BONES
Dogs enjoy chewing large marrow bones, and this is good for them, especially when teething. It keeps the jaws exercised and the teeth clean. The sort of bones you give is very important. Beef shin or knuckle (marrow) bones are best as they will not splinter. Never give your dog sharp, little bones, such as chicken or rabbit bones, nor bones you have been cooking for a very long time. They can splinter and cause internal injury.

CHOOSING A FEEDING METHOD
When deciding which method of feeding to adopt, it is wise to take stock of all the different methods, and then decide which diet sounds right for your dog and lifestyle. Some people have lots of time and prefer to do all the cutting, weighing and working out themselves. Others prefer to follow a diet plan and everything is sorted out for them. It is also important to bear in mind that we can do more harm than good with supplements when over-used routinely.

How do you know you are giving your dog the right diet? Look at your dog; you do not want your Golden Retriever to be too fat, nor too thin. You want to see a glossy coat, an elastic-feeling skin, bright eyes, and a dog that is ready for anything. There is no cheap, magic way to feed your dog, but this does not mean that feeding your dog should be a very expensive item. The time and thought you put in to getting the right diet will pay dividends throughout your dog's life.

EXERCISE
Exercising and grooming your Golden Retriever also play their part in producing a fit dog. Grooming is dealt with in the chapter on Grooming and Showing. Exercising your dog is, I think, one of the best aspects of dog ownership – but it must be done regularly, not only when the sun shines!

Many authors of dog books suggest an almost impossible amount of exercise. However, I would recommend a routine of forty-five minutes morning and afternoon, entailing a steady walk on the lead on a hard surface at first, followed by a good run and then a 'sniff around' off the lead in a park or fields. I do not consider that going shopping constitutes sufficient exercise, and I also find that no matter how large your garden is, dogs do not exercise themselves.

GROOMING
Whether you have show dog or pet dog, grooming is an essential part of keeping your Golden Retriever in top-class condition. It is a good idea to start a grooming routine with your puppy, right from the start. You will not have a lot of coat to cope with at this stage, but it is important to teach the pup to stand and lie still. My dogs queue up for the pleasure of being groomed – and that is

Your Golden Retriever will benefit from regular grooming. The hound-glove is a useful item of equipment.

Steve Nash.

what it should be, an enjoyable experience for the dog. This will not be the case if you leave too long between grooming sessions, so that 'fur mats' form in the trouser feathering, under the ears and elbows, which are most uncomfortable for the dog.

GROOMING EQUIPMENT
It is easier to groom a dog on a special table, designed specifically for the purpose. These vary in price, according to the number of gadgets that the table is equipped with. It is also quite easy to convert an old kitchen table, using non-slip rubber matting on the top. However, this is cumbersome to store as it cannot be folded away like the purpose-built grooming table.

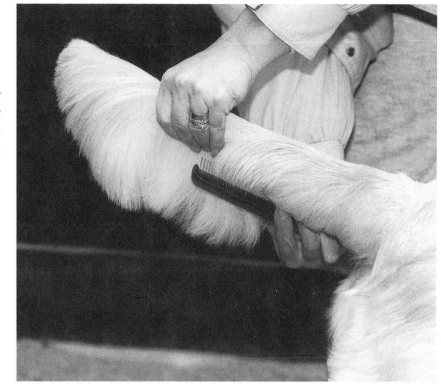

A fine-toothed comb is needed to remove any tangles from the feathering.

Steve Nash.

You will need a metal comb, specially made for dogs. The best type to buy is a good, general-purpose comb which has two sections with wide and narrow teeth. The narrow teeth are used for going over the coat after you have completed a first combing, using the wide section. The wide teeth are particularly useful for taking out any tangles in the feathering.

You will need a good-quality brush, known as a Slicka or Universal, and using this from the base of the coat upwards means that you have no ungroomed areas. A hound glove is very useful item of equipment. The hand fits inside, and it has fine wire on one side and material on the other. After a session with the wire side, you can add a final shine to the coat by using the material side. You can also buy an ordinary brush with stiff bristles to use especially for the feathering.

Grooming should be a daily ritual, and it does not need to take very long. You should also check that ears, eyes and teeth are clean. It also gives you the opportunity to find out if your dog has any lumps or bumps, cuts or scratches, and to make sure that your dog is not harbouring any visitors in the coat. Just as the cleanest child can pick up hair-nits, dogs can, in the same way, pick up external parasites. These must be eliminated by using sprays and shampoos. The grooming ritual also shows up skin conditions before they get a hold and your vet has to be brought in. Show dogs obviously need more thorough grooming sessions, which involves trimming your Golden Retriever (See Chapter 9: The Show Ring).

BATHING

Bathing a pet dog once a year is sufficient. However, it may be necessary if your dog has rolled in something noxious or when a bitch has finished her season. If coat-casting is very bad, you may feel a bath will loosen what is left of the coat and you can have a good comb out of the hair. Dogs that are being shown look better if they are bathed a few days before the show.

For the pet owner who is giving an annual bath, you can attach a spray to the taps in the kitchen and pass this through the window and wash outside on a concrete surface. If you have a hot and cold tap outside, attach your spray on to your hosepipe – but remember, *do not* wash outside if the weather is very cold. If this is the case, you will have to use the family bath, and wash it out well afterwards. Check that the temperature of the water is neither too hot nor too cold, and use a specially formulated dog shampoo, insecticidal, if necessary. Follow the instructions, and make sure you rinse the coat well, so that no shampoo remains. Rub your dog dry with a towel, or use a hair-dryer, making sure it is not blowing too hot. Finish off by giving your dog a good comb through, so that the coat dries nice and flat.

Chapter Four

HOUSING

In this Chapter you can, hopefully, learn from the mistakes I have made, and also read about the plus points I have seen in other kennels – ideas proven and tried and well worth incorporating into a kennel plan. I, personally, feel that one, two or three Golden Retrievers are ideally kept in your home, with you, because as a breed they thrive with human companionship. They easily acquire house manners when taught and quickly they become an integral part of the household. So please, if you are only having one Golden Retriever never, never kennel a dog alone – for to leave a dog with no companionship is cruel. However, beware of giving rooms over to a large number of dogs if you live in a large house. It becomes difficult to keep down 'doggy smells', and all you are doing is using rooms as kennels. It is a different matter if you use a utility room for whelping or for putting house pets in to dry off, if they are very wet and muddy.

PUPPY ACCOMMODATION
When you first bring your puppy home, it is important to provide a special place where the pup can sleep at night and rest in the daytime. This area should be contain the puppy in safety on the occasions when you have to go out. To build this 'safe area' you can buy metal mesh puppy panels (one-inch mesh), and if these are clipped together they will form a play pen. Your play pen can consist of four panels, or you can add more panels to make it larger. This structure will be strong enough to stay upright if the puppy jumps up against it. If you are handy at do-it-yourself, or if you have a DIY expert in the family, you can make your own framework of wood and fill the middle with sheets of strong metal mesh; about one inch is ideal (2.5cm) because the holes must not be so large that the puppy's head or paws can go through and get stuck. The panels should be 3ft 6ins by 3ft (105cm by 90cm).

While the puppy is learning to be clean, especially through the night, leave newspapers in one corner. The play pen is also very useful as a place where the puppy can rest or play if you have visitors who do not like dogs, or if the hustle and bustle of the household means that, temporarily, the puppy is underfoot.

Dog crates are a standard item of equipment in the USA, and they are becoming increasingly popular elsewhere. A dog crate is a large box, made of welded steel, that can be folded down. They come in different sizes, and you must buy the size that will be suitable for an adult Golden Retriever. I find a dog crate is very useful if you plan to take your dog away with you to hotels, motels or caravans, as they are ideal for providing a safe and familiar sleeping place in a strange environment. The size for an adult Golden Retriever is 41ins by 25ins by 27ins (104cm by 63.5cms by 67.5cm). These crates can also be used inside an estate car, hatchback or van.

A play pen is an invaluable item of equipment when you are rearing puppies.

R. Dixon.

BUILDING KENNELS

THE KENNELS
If you plan to breed or show on a scale that makes it impossible to keep all your Golden Retrievers in the house, or if you wish to plan for a future when you will have more dogs, you will need to build kennels or adapt existing outbuildings. This is an expensive business, and it is better to take a little longer to work out a plan, taking into consideration your plans for the future. For instance, are going to keep to a single sex, or if you mix the sexes what will you do when bitches are in season?

   The first decision you have to make is, where are you going to site the kennels? Here, I can give you the benefit of a mistake I once made. If you think you will put the kennels at the end of a long garden, where the dogs can see the back door and see all the activity that goes on in the house, or where they can see down the drive to the front gate – DON'T! Although not great barkers, Golden Retrievers naturally want to join in all activities, and if they are prevented from doing so, they are likely to start barking – and it will not be long before your neighbours start complaining.

BUILDING MATERIALS
What is the best material to use for building kennels so that you get a lifetime of use, with easy, inexpensive maintenance? I would recommend concrete blocks, painted with cement paint, which you can paint over again with more cement paint increasing the waterproofing. Brick and breeze blocks are also good for building kennels. Wood is often used if you buy the kennels made up, and this type comes as a single kennel, a double kennel, or a kennel range. One problem with wood seems to be the Golden Retriever's ability and desire to crunch it. Wooden doors and bed-edges have to be lined with steel. If you buy wood, the inside of the kennel must be lined with hardboard

to provide extra insulation. Garden sheds can also be adapted – again, you must ensure they are lined. All kennels must have windows that open, but these must be covered in wire mesh.

KENNEL CONSTRUCTION

If you plan to kennel your Golden Retrievers in pairs, the kennel-size you need is 8ft by 5ft (240cm by150cm). It is important to bear in mind with any kennel that you must be able to stand upright for ease when cleaning. The floor should be constructed of smooth concrete (smooth concrete dries quicker than rough), and fitted with a drain. If you have a wooden building, the floor will be made of wood, and this will need to be covered with a heavy-duty lino or some such floor covering that makes cleaning easier.

It is a good idea to keep a fine layer of sawdust on the kennel floor as it makes it easier to lift up mess and it absorbs liquid, although I find that kennel dogs are as clean as house-trained dogs, if they are properly looked after. The drain should be fitted with a cover so that it does not become blocked with sawdust. I know some breeders do not leave sawdust down all the time. Instead, when the dogs are waiting in the yard to be exercised, sawdust that has been sprayed with a very good disinfectant, is lightly thrown over the floor, but when the dogs return from exercise and before they go back in the kennel, the sawdust is brushed up and the floor is clean and dry.

BEDS

I favour installing a sleeping bench which is raised off the floor. This should be roomy, with enough space for the dogs to stretch out. As Golden Retrievers are reasonably tough dogs, they do not really need artificial heat in their kennels, as long as they are kept draught-free. The exceptions are puppies, when a heat lamp is required, and if you have a very old kennel dog a little extra heat may be appreciated in the depths of winter. For this reason, I suggest you install an electric point in each kennel. A useful tip is to construct sleeping benches with a 'roof' or lid to them. This should be high enough so the dog can stand up, but as hot air rises, the heat the dog gives off is not lost, and is there to keep the dog warm. The lid can be clipped up against the wall when the bed is being cleaned out. Some breeders prefer to use individual plastic dog beds for all their inmates – and it seems the dogs always know which is their own bed.

BEDDING

The choice of bedding materials is vast, and they all have advantages and disadvantages – it is a matter of finding out which you find most convenient. The fleecy, machine-washable fabric is ideal for house dogs, but in kennels the dogs tend to drag it out into the run and play around with it. In no time you find this type of bedding needs washing every day, plus a clean piece every night – enough to make the manufacturers' rub their hand with glee!

Shredded paper, which is soft and white and is sold in bales, is becoming very popular among breeders. It has many plus points, but some Goldens seem to spend a lot of time retrieving small amounts out into the run, and it has to be changed quite frequently. Wood-shavings and wood-wool have their devotees, but you must watch out that the bedding does not get down the drains. Straw is not so readily available nowadays, and the sprays used on the crop when it is growing can lead to skin itch on some dogs. The other disadvantages are that straw soon becomes broken, and it creates a lot of dust. It loses its buoyancy, and it must be kept well topped up.

Obviously you will need facilities for getting rid of the used bedding (except the fleecy washable sort) so you should allow space for an incinerator. Straw could be mulched down and used for gardening purposes.

KENNEL RUNS

Each kennel should have a run attached to it. This does not have to be very large – 22ft by 10ft (7m x 3m) – is sufficient for the dogs to move around and play. I prefer the run to be covered, and see-through roof panels are ideal for this purpose. The run should be constructed of a half-brick wall, then wire mesh, which allows plenty of air to circulate. You will need a door from the kennel into the covered run. You can have a specially constructed door which has a part that can be dropped down to close it, if necessary. The floor surface in your covered run should be smooth concrete, as it dries quickly. There should be a drain for cleaning out, and a tap-point in each run comes in very useful.

On the bottom wall you will need another door that leads out into a large uncovered concrete run, or a large grass run – an area where the dogs can run and stretch their legs. If you decide on grass, it is advisable to have paving slabs around all gateways and along the edges of the run, otherwise it can become very muddy. Some people buy large amounts of gravel and have it tipped around the gate etc., but unless the gravel goes on to a hard base the constant moving of the dogs will work it down through the mud. Never let your dog lie on concrete; supply wooden pallets or platforms for the dog to lie on in the daytime.

STOOL-EATING

The correct name for this unpleasant habit is coprophagia. There are many theories as to why dogs indulge in this, the most common being that there is something lacking in the diet. My advice is never to leave faeces about in the yard or garden, and so the 'temptation' never arises.

THE KENNEL RANGE

You should always plan to have your kennel kitchen, food and bedding store and puppy facilities in one range. If I could start from scratch, I think the ideal format is a circle. Within the middle of the circle would be the kitchen, store, grooming area, and whelping room, and coming out like spokes would be the kennels and their runs. This layout means that wherever you are working the dogs can see you – and you can see them. The chain-linking between the runs should be at least 6ft high (180cm) and sunk into the ground or fastened into concrete to stop any 'diggers' leaving the runs.

How you decide to allocate your dogs in the kennels is a matter of personal preference. Some breeders put a dog and a bitch in together, but when the bitch is in season and they are separated, the dog can fret and go off his food. Others put males together, and females together, or they can live very much en famille. However, if you keep dogs and bitches there must be accommodation for the males where they cannot see nor smell the in-season bitch, otherwise they will probably go off their food and irritate with barking and whining.

Each kennel can be fitted with an automatic water bowl, similar to the type used for cattle. They can be very useful as youngsters can spend a lot of time learning to 'swim' in the metal water bowls. Some kennels tie buckets up on the wall, but this must be done securely, so there is no risk of accidents.

To summarise: if you think you are going to need kennels, try to see as many in use as you can – commercial as well as private. Your top priorities are the welfare of the dogs and the ease of running a busy kennel. If your dogs are going to win they have to be in top condition, and this is where housing plays such an important part.

Chapter Five

HEALTH CARE

FINDING A VET

The Golden Retriever is a healthy, hardy dog but you will, of course, have a certain amount of contact with a veterinary surgeon, even if it is only when your puppy is inoculated and returns for annual boosters, so the choice of vet is very important. New owners tend to go on recommendations: often asking the puppy's breeder for advice. Make sure you choose a vet who is reasonably close to your home, for nowadays vets do not do as many house visits, and so you will have to travel to your vet's surgery. The aim is for your dog to build up a good relationship with the vet, and so try to ensure the first visit is as pleasant as possible. Remember your veterinary surgeon wants to build up a good working relationship with you, and you must have full confidence in your vet's abilities.

There are many forms of canine veterinary insurance. In the UK some breeders insure a litter, and you may choose to carry on with that policy or choose a new scheme. Veterinary care is not cheap, but it is essential.

GENERAL CARE

FIRST-AID KIT

It's a good idea to make up a canine first-aid kit, which should be kept in a box, and clearly labelled. It should include:
Tweezers
Curved and straight sharp scissors
A roll of bandage
A roll of adhesive bandage
Disinfectant
Cotton wool (cotton)
Antiseptic cream
Antiseptic powder

GIVING MEDICATION

TABLETS

Open your dog's mouth, with your left hand, by tilting the head upwards and opening the jaw. Hold the tablet between thumb and index finger of the right hand, and push the tablet as far back

Sh. Ch. Amirene King Eider of Davern, bred by Mrs M. Wood, owned by Mr and Mrs C.R. Lowe.

The Golden Retriever is a hardy breed, and with the right care and diet, it will look the picture of health.

David Dalton.

as possible over the back of the tongue. Close the mouth, hold it closed and gently stroke the throat to make the dog swallow. Some tablets are designed to be palatable and the dog will eat them readily. Tablets can be crushed in the food, but check the dog has consumed all the tablet.

MEDICINE
Small plastic syringes can be bought from the chemist, and this makes the task much easier. Pour the correct amount of liquid into the syringe, insert your finger inside the dog's lips, lift the lip and squirt through the teeth. If you are using a spoon, open the dog's mouth and put medicine on to the tongue.

INOCULATIONS
There are four diseases that can kill dogs. They are:
1. Distemper (Hard Pad is a form of distemper).
2.Canine Hepatitis
4. Leptospiral Jaundice
5. Parvovirus Infection.

Dogs can be protected against all these diseases and booster programmes will be worked out by your vet. Most boarding kennels will insist on seeing up-to-date vaccination certificates before they accept a dog. Dogs can also be inoculated against Kennel Cough. This is an infectious form of bronchitis, and an affected dog will have a harsh cough. Dogs can become infected by breathing in infected airborne particles. The disease can be long-lasting, and although it is not life-threatening to adults, it can pose a danger to very young puppies and very old dogs. The quicker you seek veterinary attention, the more rapid the recovery.

A family portrait of Goldens (left to right): Sh.Ch. Sinnhein Minutemaid and her sons Sh. Ch. Sinnhein Toerag of Kilgraston and Sh.Ch. Sinnhein Sebastian.

The Golden Retriever has a few hereditary problems, but with careful breeding, these can be eliminated.

COMMON AILMENTS

ANAL GLANDS
These glands are located on either side of the anus, and sometimes they become filled with secretion. Often the dog will rub the area along the ground. The vet will empty these, relieving the dog's discomfort.

BEE OR WASP STINGS
If you can see the sting, pull it out with tweezers, and apply anti-histamine ointment. Monitor the amount of swelling. If swelling is in mouth or throat, seek immediate veterinary attention, as breathing or swallowing can be badly affected.

CANKER
This is an inflammation of the lining of the external ear. Symptoms include shaking the head, scratching and rubbing the ear, an accumulation of wax, reddening of the ear-flap, and a smell. Do not poke around the ear yourself, you can do irreparable harm. Veterinary treatment is needed before the condition worsens. Wounds on the ear can take a long time to heal because of the continuous shaking and poor blood supply to this area.

DIARRHOEA
This can be an early indication of an unbalanced diet, and can often be cured with an investigation into what is being fed, and adding a handful of bran, bought from a health food shop or a pet store. In humans, bran can act as a laxative, but in dogs it has the opposite effect. If the diarrhoea is persistent, there is likely to be another cause, so you should consult your vet.

PARASITES

ENDOPARASITES (WORMS)
These are parasites that live within the body. The two common to the dog are Toxocara Canis (roundworms) and Dipylidium Caninum (tapeworm). Always check that the puppy you are buying has been wormed at least twice with an effective wormer before eight weeks of age.

ROUNDWORMS
The roundworm is a white worm 3-6 ins (7-15 cms) in length. When a bitch is pregnant, the release of hormones starts off the roundworm larvae. Some will go into the uterus and into the developing puppies, and, therefore, we can assume that all puppies and their dams will have some worms. Heavy worm infestation will cause breathing problems, diarrhoea, retarded growth, and an unhealthy appearance. In extreme cases, this can be life-threatening, and, as puppies are handled by children, it is important to take sensible precautions. Ask your vet for advice on suitable worming treatments.

TAPEWORMS
The segmented tapeworm occurs in the small intestine of dogs and can measure up to 20 ins (50 cms) in length. The worm attaches itself to the wall of the intestine, and its long segmented body contains maturing eggs in each segment. You can see these individual segments in faeces, looking like cucumber seeds, or when dried they look like grains of rice. Fleas are a necessary part of the tapeworm's lifecycle, and so you must keep your dog free from this external parasite as well. The signs of tapeworm infestation are diarrhoea, poor condition, and poor growth. The vet will prescribe an effective worming treatment.

ECTOPARASITES
These are parasites that live on or in the skin, and they are probably the main cause of skin disease in dogs. They include:
1. Fleas
2. Lice
3. Ticks
4. Mange mites

FLEAS: These are long, brown wingless insects that run quickly over the skin. This movement causes irritation so that the dog scratches constantly. Regular treatment with baths, powders and sprays is needed to overcome them and to stop reinfestation. Remember also to treat the environment. Life cycle is completed off the dog.

LICE: These feed on the skin, laying eggs in the hair. They are light-brown, fat, wingless insects moving slowly and laying eggs (nits). Dogs scratch constantly at the parts where the lice are to be found. A severe infestation can cause anaemia in young puppies. Regular treatment with an insecticide is required.

TICKS: These are brownish-white, rounded insects, and when full of blood they are the size of a bean. Ticks attach to a dog by their heads, which are buried in the skin. They can be removed by soaking in surgical spirit, which loosens the head, enabling you to remove the tick in entirety. If the head is not removed, it could start up an infection.

MANGE MITES: These are usually invisible to the naked eye. The vet will diagnose which mange mite is causing the trouble, and will then prescribe the correct treatment.

PUPPY GLAND DISEASE (JUVENILE PYODERMA)

This can occur in puppies under four months of age, and cases have occurred in Golden Retrievers. It is thought to be a temporary failure of the immune system, and is an inflammation of the skin and glands in the head. You notice large, painful swellings around the eyes and lips and on the head, and they may spread over the whole body. These swellings will eventually burst and the pus drains out. A course of antibiotic seems to work well. If you do use medication, although the puppy should recover, there may be scarring. This condition can be mistaken for an eye infection, so it is worth mentioning the possibility of PGD to your vet.

PYOMETRA

This condition is caused by accumulation of large amounts of fluid in the uterus, usually occurring one or two months after bitch has been in season. The signs are: excessive drinking, frequent passing of urine, and raised temperature. With Open Pyometra, there will be a thick, brown foul-smelling discharge from the vulva. Seek veterinary help at once – immediate surgery to remove the uterus and ovaries may be needed in order to save the bitch's life.

INHERITED CONDITIONS

CATARACT

This is an opacity of the lens in the eye. There are a number of causes of cataract, but hereditary cataract occurs in some breeds including the Golden Retriever. Progressive Retinal Atrophy (PRA) is the progressive destruction of the retina (the light sensitive tissue at the back of the eye). No treatment is possible and no cure found in Golden Retrievers.

In the UK, the Kennel Club, in conjunction with the British Veterinary Association, has an eye scheme which aims to control and eventually to eliminate hereditary eye diseases in Golden Retrievers. In order to achieve this, it is advised that all Golden Retrievers should be eye-tested from twelve months of age until they die. Your vet will tell you where a panel vet is examining eyes, or your area breed club may schedule a day when a panel vet comes and examines eyes at a convenient venue. Bitches should never be bred from without having up-to-date eye certificates, and the same is true for dogs being used at stud. When you buy a puppy, check that the sire and dam have up-to-date eye certificates.

In the USA, eye examinations should be made by a Board Certified Veterinary Ophthalmologist. Dogs examined and found to be free of hereditary eye disease can be registered with the Canine Eye Registration Foundations (CERF). CERF then issue the dog with a number.

ENTROPION

Eyelid and eyelash problems may occur in Golden Retrievers, some with an hereditary basis, and some due to other factors. Entropion and Ectropion refer to the turning-in or turning-out of the eyelids. Trichiasis and dilstichiasis involve eyelashes or hairs rubbing on and irritating the eye. Surgery may be needed to correct these problems. It is a simple operation, but affected dogs should not be bred from, and in the USA such dogs are ineligible to be shown under AKC rules.

EPILEPSY

To many people, epilepsy and fits are synonymous. This leads to complications because a fit is a symptom, while epilepsy is usually considered to be a disease or condition. A fit can be a symptom of many different conditions, eg. distemper or brain tumour, and these have no hereditary significance. When a fit occurs, it may only last a minute. The form it usually takes is a rigid period followed by shaking and spasm of the muscles, and then involuntary paddling with the paws. When the fit subsides, the dog lies quietly for a little time, then struggles up and wanders around on weak legs, sometimes banging into furniture and walls.

However, within half-an-hour it is impossible to know the dog has had a fit. It is, therefore, no use telephoning your vet and asking for a house visit, as the dog will most probably have returned to normal by the time the vet arrives. The best thing to do is to make a note of what has happened, noting times, and then give these particulars to your vet. Tests will be carried out, hopefully resulting in accurate diagnosis. Treatment is available, and in some cases this may result in a complete cure.

Conditions that can have fits as a symptom include primary epilepsy, and that is significant with regard to heredity. The mechanism of the heredity is not understood, and so it is not advisable to breed from an animal with primary epilepsy, nor to mate together the sire and dam of that dog on a subsequent occasion. There is no evidence at the moment to show that related dogs will either have or carry primary epilepsy as a matter of fact. There is no means of detecting carriers. One of the most important aspects in these cases is correct diagnosis.

HIP DYSPLASIA

A joint is the area where two or more bones come together to form the likeness of a 'hinge'. The hip is a ball and socket joint, which allows for rotation in movement to occur. In cases of hip dysplasia, changes occur in the socket (Acetabulum), and/or to the head of the femur, so that the joint does not function properly. This malfunction is influenced by hereditary and other factors. Golden Retrievers suffer from hip dysplasia, and should be X-rayed and scored. In the UK the X-rays are taken after twelve months of age, in the USA it is after 24 months of age. In America the X-ray plates are submitted to the Orthopedic Foundation for Animals (OFA) in Columbia, Missouri, and they assign permanent OFA registry numbers. In the UK the plates are assessed by a panel of experts and then scored.

For many years, the well-known geneticist, Dr M.B. Willis, has been sent the results and has produced data. The breed average for Golden Retrievers is just over 18. Dr Willis also has produced progeny-tested data, and you can monitor the stud dogs which have produced low hip scores and the dogs producing high hip scores in their offspring, and which dogs have improved hip scores against the scores of the bitches they have been mated to.

Both dogs and bitches should be tested before they are used in a breeding programme, and you should never buy a puppy from parents that have not been tested. Admittedly, HD is only one factor to consider, but it is a condition that affects the animal physically, so it is much easier to do the right thing in the beginning. HD can only be diagnosed by X-ray, not by looking at the dog's movement. Sometimes, strangely enough, dogs with incorrect movement can have a good score, and vice versa. Young dogs with HD may have a swaying movement when walking and stiffness after exercise. Older dogs usually end up with osteoarthritis, but many dogs with quite bad HD live long lives, without inconvenience. As long as these animals are excluded from breeding programmes, they will be perfectly suitable as companion dogs. Most countries have HD schemes in operation, and some countries have breeding restrictions based on hip scores.

OSTEOCHONDRITIS DISSECANS (OCD)

Many joints can be affected by this condition, usually the shoulder, elbow, hock or stifle joints. Small bits of cartilage separate from the bone,causing pain and discomfort. Following X-rays, surgery may be required. Signs occur between four to eight months, and the condition progresses gradually, with lameness that worsens after exercise, followed by a stiffness in movement. The causes are various – over-exercising youngsters, high jumping when too young, over-feeding of additives. It can be inherited and made worse by the stated factors.

EUTHANASIA

This is one of the hardest decisions you will ever have to make, and it is awesome to have the power of life or death. However, when the dog you have loved, who has given you love and devotion, has reached a stage where the quality of life has deteriorated, the decision has to be made. You should stay with your dog when the vet gives an injection, and your pet will die in peace, and with complete dignity.

Chapter Six

EARLY TRAINING

SOCIALISATION

Training your Golden Retriever puppy to fit into your family life is a very rewarding task. If you have young children, you must educate them right from the beginning not to think of the puppy as a mechanical toy to be played with and then thrown away. A puppy is a living creature, and children must learn to have a responsible attitude towards this new member of the family. Anyone who buys a puppy must take on the task of house training; the chewing stage when the puppy is teething must be endured, and nowadays there is an awareness of potential behavioural problems and how to avoid them.

Puppies have to learn to relate to people and other dogs. We call this socialisation, and the term for becoming accustomed to a range of environments is called habituation. Scientific research has shown that the important socialisation and habituation period is up to twelve to fourteen weeks old. As puppies should remain with the breeder until they are at least seven weeks old, the breeder should do as much socialisation/habituation as they can – and then it is over to you!

One of the great problems against early socialisation and habituation is the requirements of the vaccination programme. Puppies must be kept away from sources of infection until the programme is complete, which is usually after twelve weeks of age. This means you have to keep your puppy within your own boundaries during that vulnerable period.

In order to appreciate the situation more fully, it is important to understand how the vaccination programme works. In fact, it starts when the bitch has her litter, and she passes antibodies (immunity) to infectious diseases via her milk to her puppies. The level of the immunity gradually reduces, so that by twelve weeks most puppies have lost their effective immunity to infection. However, the problem is that the level of immunity diminishes at different rates from one puppy to another. It is, therefore, usually recommended that the vaccination programme should be started at twelve weeks.

Nowadays, you can have the programme started at an earlier age, and this you can discuss with your vet. One very important thing to remember, whenever or whatever vaccination programme your puppy follows, an annual booster is required from the vet for the rest of your dog's life.

From five to seven weeks, before the puppies leave the nest, they learn canine socialisation with their littermates. Socialisation with humans is from the eighth to the twelfth week, starting when the puppy leaves both brothers and sisters, and moves outside the mother's influence. As the puppy grows, from the thirteenth to the sixteenth week, this is the time to build up love and security, establishing an environment of confidence, supervised play with children (the children supervised as well as puppy), and introducing a system of gentle discipline.

A Golden Retriever has a lot to learn in the first few months of its life.

Steve Nash.

CHEWING

Puppies do need to chew, and this is particularly the case between four and six months of age when milk teeth are being replaced by adult teeth. During this time do not leave your puppy alone, to find things to chew, which can either cause damage or be potentially dangerous. A puppy left alone in the kitchen is quite likely to start chewing electric wires, which could have disastrous results. I do not give my puppies old shoes or clothes to chew, for a puppy cannot tell the difference between old and new, and will not realise which must not be touched.

You can buy chew items from your pet store, and large marrow bones from your butcher. If you find your puppy is chewing something forbidden, take it from your pup saying "No", and then replace the forbidden object with a chew stick, and also give lots of praise.

HOUSE TRAINING YOUR PUPPY

Puppies, like babies, have no control and need to relieve themselves many times. They need to go outside when they wake up, straight after eating, after an active play, and when they start to wander round sniffling with an expression on their face that you soon get used to! When you take your puppy out, you must stay in attendance until the pup 'performs', and then give lots of praise.

It is a good idea to think of a phrase to use, which then becomes fixed in the puppy's mind, and is associated with the act. This trigger word or phrase can be very useful if you are in a situation away from home and you want the puppy to oblige. I say "be a good dog", but any phrase, as long as it has the mind association, will do. You can train your puppy to use a certain part of the outside area if you always go to it. The operative word is 'you', for *you* must physically take the puppy out, never just open the door and put the pup out. If you do that, the puppy will invariably come in and toilet inside, the moment you open the door.

The very young puppy will toilet almost hourly, and once or twice during the night. As the puppy grows older, gains bladder control, and starts to understand being house trained, the trips outside will become fewer. Soon you will not need to go with the puppy, who will soon ask by crying or barking to go out. Never punish the puppy for a mistake in the house, unless you catch the puppy in the act of doing it. If you do catch the puppy, say "No" firmly, pick the puppy up, and go to the usual place in the garden, and then give lots of praise if the puppy then does the toileting in the correct place. Punishing a puppy after a mistake is useless, you will only succeed in confusing your puppy. Never hit the puppy, and never rub the pup's nose in the mess.

PLAY PEN AND CRATE TRAINING
If you have a single Golden Retriever puppy, or a single adult, an outdoor kennel is completely unsuitable. However, a puppy who is either coming to live in a house as the only dog or is joining other dogs, needs a safe area to sleep in. You can either make a safe area (no electric sockets) with puppy metal panels, turning it into a play pen, or you can buy a dog crate. The crate must be bought for the size of the adult Golden Retriever. A dog crate consists of a rectangular box with a top, bottom and door, made of aluminium or metal wire; it folds down to panels for ease of moving without the dog. A quality crate will last for a long time, and if you use a piece of fleecy blanket it makes an ideal 'den' – a place the puppy will choose to go to.

Pet owners often say, at first, that they do not want to put a puppy in a cage. However, the benefits of a crate depend on how it is used. A dog should never be confined to a crate for long periods. In fact, it should never be used by anyone who has to leave a dog for a long period of time. I would suggest that a puppy is never left for longer than an hour in a crate. Once the puppy accepts the crate as a sleeping den, and as a play pen for short confinement, the crate can be used at those times when puppies can be great nuisances, such as when you are cooking, at mealtimes, when the children have friends to play, or if you ever have non-doggy guests or workmen in the house. If you take your dog away from home, the crate becomes a home from home. It can also be very useful during house training, but it should never be used as a punishment cell.

Your puppy will be quick to accept the crate as a safe haven, particularly if you make it comfortable with a piece of fleecy material or a blanket, and leave some favourite toys in it. The first few times you put the puppy in the crate, you will probably hear some howls of protest. Your puppy does not want to be left alone and wants to get back to you. Do not give in and take the puppy out. Wait until the puppy has settled down, then after a short time go back, take the pup out of the crate and give lots of praise.

It is a good idea to feed your puppy in the pen or crate, remembering to take the pup straight out for toileting. As regards house training, the crate can be a useful aid, as at night you can leave newspaper at one end, and the puppy will get used to using this, rather than soiling the sleeping area. It is important to establish a routine, putting the puppy away to sleep when you are not actually playing or involved with the puppy.

You must also teach your puppy to get used to being left alone for longer periods. Puppies who are not accustomed to being left alone on a regular basis can suffer from an anxiety, and this is generally shown in three ways: destructiveness, howling or barking, or making messes in the house. Therefore, the puppy must learn to be left in the play pen/crate for an hour, while you are in other parts of the house. As the puppy learns to settle, you can leave the house, going shopping etc., but at the beginning never leave your puppy for longer than an hour. If the puppy cries, do not go back; the puppy will associate crying with your returning.

When the puppy is older and you go out, remember that even a house-trained dog must have the opportunity to go out, and so you must arrange for family or friends to let the dog out if you cannot. No adult dog should be left in a crate for more than two and a half hours.

COLLAR TO LEAD TRAINING

You can start this at home before the vaccination programme is complete. Puppy collars are lightweight and only designed to be used on the puppy, not on the adult dog. Measure the puppy's neck, and your local pet store will sell you the right size collar. At first, just put the collar on for ten to fifteen minutes while the puppy is running around. Most puppies will try to scratch it off to begin with, but if you gradually increase the length of time the collar is on, your puppy will soon forget it is on. When your Golden Retriever is ready for a proper collar, I would suggest that you choose one made of nylon-web or a rolled leather collar. Wide, flat leather can break the neck hair and make an ugly mark. Remember, you need an identification disc on the dog's collar with your name, address and telephone number. Later on, you can discuss with your vet whether you want to have your dog tattooed in case of loss or theft.

You need a lightweight lead for a puppy, but when you graduate to the adult collar you will need to get a matching leather or material lead. A retractable flexible lead (15-30 ft) is very useful for those occasions when you cannot let the dog off the lead. Never buy a choke chain to use as a collar. They are for training only, and must never be left on a dog at other times.

Once your puppy is used to the lightweight collar, attach the lead, and encourage your puppy to walk alongside you. At first, you may find you have a bucking bronco, putting up all manner of resistance. If this happens, stop, hold the puppy and say "no" firmly, and start again. At first the lesson should only be for a few minutes, gradually building up. You often find that when you go out of your own garden, the puppy will be so interested in what is going on, you will find your pup walking beautifully. It often helps if you have another dog, for the puppy will walk quietly alongside the older dog.

BUILDING UP CONFIDENCE

From the moment you first bring your puppy home, use the name you have chosen on all occasions. When your puppy responds and comes to you, give lots of praise and loving, then allow the pup to wander off. I sometimes offer a reward – a small tidbit – when the puppy comes, reinforcing the association in the puppy's mind of name and response. Before the vaccination programme is complete you can take your puppy in the car, and if you carry your pup you can go visiting friends and relations. However, you must check that any dog you are likely to meet is up to date with inoculations.

Accustom your puppy to lots of visitors, to the postman, milkman, refuse collectors. Get your puppy used to all the domestic sounds– the vacuum cleaner, washing machine, etc. – just let your puppy get used to them gradually. If you have a cat, introduce your puppy under control. The cat will probably keep well out of the puppy's way (usually high up) until they are used to each other. If you have another dog, introductions should take place in the garden. They will soon find their own level, especially if your puppy is put into the playpen/crate periodically at first, so that they have a time apart. Obviously, you must also make sure that the other dog does not feel pushed to one side by the puppy. It is important to stop the puppy play-biting at an early stage. Puppies play physical games with their littermates and pester their mother, with the result that as they grow up, adults become intolerant of their very sharp teeth. You must teach your puppy by giving the command "No" firmly, and pushing the puppy away from you. The pup must learn that hard mouthing or play-biting is not allowed, and biting brings the opposite of attention.

TAKING YOUR PUPPY OUT

Golden Retriever puppies do not need huge amounts of exercise. Most puppies will enjoy playing in the garden and in the house, and you can build up the outside exercise gradually. By now, your puppy should be walking well on the lead and is ready to socialise with other dogs. This does not mean running around madly, and being chased by dogs in the park. If the other dogs have not been trained and are aggressive, this could teach your puppy to be frightened or aggressive.

Puppy socialisation classes are very useful. Ask your vet if there are any classes in your area. At these classes puppies learn how to read body language, and facial and vocal expression, so they can tell other dogs what they want, and they understand what other dogs are telling them. It is a bit like pre-school playschool; the atmosphere is relaxed, and after initial play sessions, exercises are gradually introduced. The emphasis is on training for fun, praising good behaviour with rewards, and avoiding hard, corrective training.

CORRECTING YOUR PUPPY

A dog most commonly becomes boisterous as a response to the environment, so keep your Golden Retriever calm. Even when your tiny puppy is the subject of much excitement with visitors and children, make sure the pup does not become over-excited. It is much kinder, and much easier, to start as you mean to go on, rather than having to correct the maturing dog for something you allowed in puppyhood.

Right from the beginning, do not let your puppy jump up. Give a firm "No", and push down so the puppy is on four feet. Do not shout at your Golden Retriever in an attempt to gain control – you cannot expect your dog to do something you have not taught. So your puppy must be trained from the beginning to sit, to lie down, and to stay at heel (see Chapter 7: Advanced Training). Use simple words of command, and make sure all members of the family use the same words.

Do not let your Golden Retriever become too dependent upon you; condition your puppy to accept some periods of isolation. Do not constantly give your attention, so that your puppy seeks this all the time with licking, pawing etc. Your Golden Retriever should get used to being shut in another room some of the time when you are at home. Give chewing articles when you go out, and remove them when you come home. Do not punish your puppy for any wrongdoing which occurred while you were out, and do not leave your puppy (or dog) for unreasonable periods of time.

The dog fits in with family life because we are like dog pack families who live in small groups. You become the dominant member of the family/pack, and this is how it should stay. It is therefore essential that you are consistent in this role. Do not feed your dog from the table, do not let your dog bite you in play. Say "No", and stop the game. You must teach your dog gently but firmly to give bones, toys etc. to you.

Do not leave your puppy or dog unattended with very small children or babies. Do not encourage your dog to bark, but if your dog is barking at something or at some noise, do not shout to stop the barking, as the dog will think you are barking as well. Do not hit your dog with your hand, the command "No", and a firm shake with your hands either side of the collar is better. Do not tell your dog off after something has been done: correction is only appropriate if you catch your dog in the act.

THE OLDER DOG

If you feel you cannot go through all the training of a baby puppy, an older puppy or a mature dog may be the answer. Many Golden Retriever Breed Clubs have rehoming schemes, and a telephone call to the Breed Club secretary will put you in touch with the appropriate organisation. Golden Retrievers are very adaptable and they can become part of a family in a very short time. The obvious advantage is that you will probably be taking on a house-trained dog who has learnt at least a few basic commands. At first there may be some confusion in the dog's mind that causes problems, but patience, care, consistency and reassurance soon overcome these early difficulties.

If you are getting a dog through a Golden Retriever rescue organisation, you will be given details of the dog's past history, and before you take on the dog, efforts will be made to determine if the dog's temperament is compatible with your lifestyle. A dog who has been neglected or mistreated needs understanding and comfort, and they will reward you with love and gratitude. With an adult dog, time must be taken to help the newcomer to adapt to a new home and a new routine. The dog's sleeping quarters, the times of meals, the permitted place for toileting, plus other 'house' rules, will all need to be taught. It is, therefore, essential in the early stages to be at home most of the time, helping to make the transition period as easy as possible.

Some near neighbours of mine took on a rescue Golden Retriever after the death of their old, much-loved Labrador Retriever. To see 'Toby' fill out in frame, acquiring a gloss on his coat and a sparkle in his eye, enjoying regular meals and walks, rabbiting in the woods and playing with other dogs, makes you appreciate the rewards of taking in a rescue dog.

*Ob. Ch. Melfricka Limelight demonstrates that
Golden Retrievers can be trained to compete at the
highest level in Obedience.*

Chapter Seven

ADVANCED TRAINING

OBEDIENCE

Border Collies, Working Sheepdogs and German Shepherd Dogs tend to dominate the competitive world of Obedience, Working Trials and Agility. However, Golden Retrievers, together with Shelties, and lately Belgian Shepherds (Sheepdogs), are also very successful in these fields. If you cannot work or train your Golden Retriever for the field, the Obedience disciplines will allow you to enjoy the pleasures of training, and will give your dog interest and stimulation. It is rather unfair to keep working or sporting breeds without allowing them to do something to stretch their considerable brains. Joan Lavender, who shows her dogs in beauty, works them in the field, and also trains them for Obedience competitions, says: "Do not be put off by people who tell you that 'sitting' at heel instead of 'standing' will ruin breed showing, as any dog capable of learning the word 'stand' can just as easily be taught the command 'sit'." Many of the Golden Retriever breed clubs put on Obedience classes at their shows, so there we can have another dual purpose aspect of the breed. I remember the first British Obedience Champion in the breed, Ob. Ch. Castlenau Pizzicato CDEX, UDEX,WDEX, owned by Mrs Needs, bred by Miss Baker, born in January 1956. He was lovely specimen of the breed, and a great ambassador.

It is desirable to enrol for a short course of Obedience, even if you wish only to compete in Agility or Working Trials, as discipline is necessary, and elementary Obedience is not usually taught at either Agility or Working Trial classes. The Kennel Club Good Citizens Test is a good standard to aim for, because, although aimed for 'pet Obedience', it is a basis from which all other working disciplines can be started.

FINDING A TRAINING CLUB
It should be realised that most people who go to Obedience classes to train their puppies and adults have, at first, no intention of entering competitive events but become so involved that they enter the events usually gradually, but often end at the top. But firstly: how to find an Obedience Club.

1. Write to your national Kennel Club. They have a list of registered clubs and they will give you the name of your nearest club and the secretary's name and address.
2. Your area Golden Retriever Breed Club might run Obedience classes.
3. Local Veterinary Surgeons and Police can often let you know the address.

If you are lucky enough to have several clubs near you, ring the secretaries and ask if you can go

Taragindi Solitaire of Melnola CDEX, UDEX, TDEX clearing the nine-foot long jump in Working Trials.

Melnola's Wild Rose CDEX, UDEX, WEEX demonstrating tracking skills with owner-handler Pat Parkinson.

and watch without your dog. There are good and not so good clubs; there are also some very competitive clubs whose trainers mostly work Collies and do not always know how to handle other breeds. If you like the kind atmosphere, lots of different breeds and very little noise from the dogs, then that is the club to sign on with. After you have spoken to the secretary, you might find there is a waiting list, but many clubs will allow you to go along without your dog while you are on the waiting list, and this means you can pick up valuable tips and start the simple beginners training at home, for when you have started your course proper you will realise that a lot of training is done at home. Going to a club will teach you what to do and will correct your faults, but the hard work is done at home.

Ideally, the club will start off with a 'baby' class for puppies just after they finish their inoculation programme. This gives puppies from three to five months the opportunity to socialise, and make a start on a few simple exercises. All the puppies are, periodically, let off the lead together to play and then called up to their owners, and it is amazing how quickly they respond. Then they do a bit more work, rewarded by tidbits, and go off to play again. In this way the puppies soon learn to enjoy and socialise with children, men, women, and perhaps a couple of trusted older dogs, so the puppies learn quickly to be petted and played with by all and sundry. They will also learn quickly to sit, stand, down, wait, come, follow off the lead. When the puppies are about five months old, owners are encouraged to join the next course class, which can lead to enrolling for the Good Citizen scheme, and passing out as a competent handler with a well-behaved dog who should fit well into the community.

OBEDIENCE COMPETITIONS

If you have got interested in training, you may wish to get involved in competitive Obedience. Again, it is important to find a good club, and with hard work and determination, there is no reason why the Golden Retriever should not compete successfully.

Dogs graduate through a series of levels, starting with fairly basic Obedience exercises, such as Heelwork, Stays and Recalls, graduating to Retrieves, Distance Control and Scent Discrimination, with all the exercises becoming increasingly difficult at every stage. The aim of the top handlers is for their dog to achieve the title Obedience Champion.

WORKING TRIALS

This is different discipline, which Golden Retrievers can also excel in. Basically, the structure of competition is organised around a dog gaining the certificates Companion Dog, Utility Dog, Tracking Dog, Working Dog and Patrol Dog in ascending order of merit. The exercises combine Obedience exercises, tracking ability, steadiness to gunshot, and agility, and it is a great achievement for both dog and handler to succeed in this demanding discipline.

AGILITY

This is a relatively new activity, which has become immensely popular in the UK. Dogs are trained to negotiate an obstacle course, which includes hurdles, an 'A' frame, a seesaw, a dog-walk weaving poles, a tunnel and a tyre. Speed is essential, coupled with accuracy, and so the fast-moving Border Collie has made this sport its own. However, other breeds, including Golden Retrievers have been successful. The most noteworthy is Charles Harvest Sun, owned by Barrie Harvey, who has a grand total of 184 wins and was in the winning team at Crufts 1993 at eight years of age. This is Charlie's story, related by Barrie's wife:

"In our house the decision to get another dog is never easy because we view them as part of the family and we all have to get on well together. However, after a lot of discussion, we decided to get another Golden Retriever as company for our older dog, Ben. Little did we know that this decision was to change our lives for ever! We read all the books and talked to people about choosing a puppy and came to the conclusion that we should look for one that was bold, confident and active. We looked at two litters but were not impressed and eventually found a litter from a pet bitch who was almost white in colour, who produced eight very nice puppies. Charlie really selected us; he was the character of the litter, very naughty, full of mischief, running in and out of the flower borders and tearing around like a lunatic!

"The house we lived in at the time was open-plan style and, to assist with the toilet training, we

Charles Harvest Sun showing of his agility skills at Crufts.

decided to keep him in the kitchen using a baby-gate (there was no door to the kitchen, merely an archway). We should have realised the shape of things to come, as he managed to get through the bars. We then put a wallpaper pasting table over the top to make an even bigger barrier, but he soon scaled this and got out to see Ben.

"At six months old the problems really began. Whenever we went out he went on the rampage, pulling things off radiators, chewing through the stereo speaker wires, pulling over the Christmas tree and eating all the decorations. On one occasion he had the washing over and swallowed five of Barrie's (unwashed) socks – four reappeared naturally, one didn't. He had this surgically removed from his lower bowel – it very nearly killed him.

"Then he started on the furniture – he literally tore the three-seater sofa into pieces! Every time we came home, even if we had only been out for fifteen minutes, there would be chewed-up foam throughout the whole house. At our wits end, we considered Retriever Rescue but decided against it, because if the dog did this to somebody else's home would they be as sympathetic as us? So we agreed to battle on. We went to see Roger Mugford, the behaviour therapist, who made several suggestions, e.g. change his routine, change his meals, etc., but he also gave us a muzzle, which stopped the chewing. He wore this for three years, every time we went out. We gave him several chances to go without it, but the old habit always returned.

"When Charlie was seven months old, the Billingshurst Dog Training Club tried to help us with the problem, and we began Obedience Classes. Unfortunately, Charlie found heelwork, recalls etc. very boring, and whilst our problems with him were not quite as bad, he was still very boisterous and strong-willed. We then discovered the club had an Agility section, and decided to give it a try. We thought it would at least give him more exercise and maybe tire him out. He seemed to enjoy himself so much, and when we were asked to join in public demonstrations, he would stop at the top of the A-frame just to make sure that everyone could see him!

"When Charlie was just over a year old we moved house to Upper Beeding in West Sussex, and, by now, he was progressing quite well with the agility training. We joined the Haywards Heath Dog Training Club's Agility Section, and Barrie and Charlie entered their first show. During the first year in competition they were eliminated or had several faults, because Charlie's natural enthusiasm greatly overshadowed his obedience! Discipline (for both Charlie and Barrie) came in the form of Tony Veal and Dalerose Dog Training School, and things started to come together at last. Barrie, by now, belonged to five agility clubs (they each trained on a different night of the week) in an effort to try and improve their technique. They were both pretty tired, but at least Charlie had stopped misbehaving himself at home.

"Charlie won Starters Agility at Bristol DTS show on 15th March 1987 (Judge – Shirley Frankcom), and Novice Agility one week later at Burridge DTC show (Judge – Val Pollock). Two months later he won Open Agility at Dartford DTC show, and suddenly he was a Senior Dog. The rest, as they say, is history. Three times at the Pedigree Chum Olympia finals (1987, 1989, 1991) – we have been told he is the only Golden Retriever to get there; two consecutive years in the winning team at Crufts, two years in the final of Barbour Pairs with partner Jackie Meader and her Charlie; starring in the television programme *Superdogs*, and numerous other TV appearances. Because Charlie is 'different' he gets a lot of extra publicity, and we are very proud of him.

"Barrie has put a lot of hard work and time into training Charlie. They currently train three nights a week and have an hour's walk on the South Downs every morning with the other three dogs. Charlie, like most other Agility dogs, likes to please his handler. He needs a bit of 'winding-up' before he goes in the ring and plenty of praise when he comes out! There is always someone around to do that. Barrie prepares very carefully for his shows and puts extra effort into the finals. He prepares very differently for the individual events to the team events and is a great believer in exploiting your strengths and overcoming the weaknesses. Whatever they do, they try to do well and to enjoy themselves. They work extremely well together, and love and respect each other. Charlie really is Barrie's 'once in a lifetime dog'.

By the way, Charlie stopped chewing the house as well!"

THE FIELD

GUNDOG CHARACTERISTICS

The Golden Retriever was evolved to do a job of work. The breed was developed to hunt and retrieve, not just to trot out forty yards and retrieve a dead bird, but to bring back runners and lightly-shot birds, to take directional command and to retrieve game which the dog has not seen fall. If you want your Golden solely to work to the gun, you are better advised to buy a puppy from proved working lines, which will enhance your chances of success.

What exactly do we mean by a dual-purpose dog? A real dual-purpose dog is one who can perform with merit in both the show ring and in the field. The last British Dual Champion in Golden Retrievers was International Dual Champion David of Westley, born June 6th 1951. The competition in both show and work is so very high nowadays that it has caused a split. On the show side, the Golden Retriever must have excellent temperament, good construction, breed type and, of course, the dog should have soundness. Show dogs tend to be much heavier in build, mostly lacking speed and biddability. Many people would argue that their dogs have biddability, until they are compared to the working-bred dog!

On the working side, looks are not important. Again, we are looking for excellent temperament, plus speed, style, game-finding ability, courage, stamina to cope with thick cover, fording fast-

Windrush Gunner shows the strength and stamina needed by the working retriever.

Graham Cox.

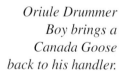

Oriule Drummer Boy brings a Canada Goose back to his handler.

Graham Cox.

flowing rivers, jumping fences and, of course, that great virtue – biddability. It is no good having a hard-headed dog in a field of roots, which is full of game. You need to have a dog that is responsive to the whistle, and who will go where the handler wishes, rather than pursuing personal desires. On the other hand, the dog must learn to hunt and to use initiative, learning to take a line on a wounded bird. Marking ability is so important and, in many ways, although Golden Retrievers are not such fast swimmers as Labrador Retrievers, the Golden's marking ability is legendary. Working Goldens are expected to fulfil the different roles which depend on the type of shooting their owners prefer.

PRE-TRAINING

Most well-known trainers of Golden Retrievers find them more sensitive than Labrador Retrievers, and more easily upset. So, if you lose your temper easily, do not try to train a Golden Retriever or any other gundog. At what age should you start training your puppy? Well, this does tend to vary with the temperament of your dog. If you have a real tough, bouncy extrovert, you can start at six months. However, if you have a very sensitive puppy, you should prolong the pre-training stage, coupled with the right sort of discipline, and you should be ready to start formal training when your dog is a year old, or even later. Remember, before training starts there has to be a real bond between puppy and trainer, and this bonding work is done at home.

BUILDING A BOND

You can start building the all-important bond with your Golden Retriever while you are waiting for the vaccination programme to be completed. Your puppy can get used to wearing a collar, and walking on a lead can be started in the garden, training the puppy to follow at the left side. Keep the lessons short; five-minute sessions are sufficient. Stop when your puppy is doing what is required – and this idea must be followed through with all your training. Always finish on a correct note. Call the puppy to you at frequent intervals, then make a great fuss and give lots of praise for coming straight to you, and let the puppy go off again. You want to try and bring the puppy up with good habits, and not to have to re-train in order to break bad habits. Another important point to remember is that hitting and terrifying a puppy gets you nowhere. A very short shake, with one hand either side of the neck, is a better way of correcting a puppy. You must always use the same word for every command, and keep the vocabulary simple.

The puppy will constantly carry articles in the pre-training stage, for natural retrieving ability will show at an early stage. Encourage this by calling your puppy to you, and then using the command word (the usual one is "dead"), and gently get the puppy to give up the article. The important word is 'gently'. You must never snatch anything away roughly, or you can ruin good delivery later on. You can do some 'baby' retrieving at this stage, using a small, soft dummy.

Start by getting your puppy's attention, and throw the dummy a few yards. The pup will dash to pick it up, and you must encourage the puppy to bring it right up to you. The best way of doing this is to bend down or kneel down, and that should make the puppy bring the dummy right up to you. If the puppy hesitates to come, turn and move away, and this usually makes the puppy dash up to you. Give lots of praise, really make your pleasure known, before taking the dummy from the puppy. At this stage, your puppy does not need a lot of retrieves. Never overdo this exercise, once you know your pup will retrieve. The basic obedience should come first with, perhaps, one retrieve at the end of the short session as a treat. If the puppy does not want to bring the dummy back, try the exercise again in a confined area, such as corridor, which does not lead anywhere except back to the trainer. I repeat, do not go on for too long. The puppy must not be allowed think it is always right to run in for something that is thrown. You really need to get to know your puppy very well, especially when the puppy can go out for short rambles, at first on the lead and then off the lead. When you are out, encourage the puppy to investigate long grass and bushes, and also get the puppy used to the car, and, an important point, which part of the car you wish the puppy to travel in! Crates are ideal for both puppies and adult dogs when in transit. Dog guards, which confine the dog to the rear of the car, are good, but check that the puppy cannot get through to you, and risk getting stuck. Play training with puppies starts almost as soon as you have them, calling them to you, letting them 'follow' your hands. Your hands play such a big part in training – all your handling in the future will be done with your whistle and hands. Remember, the art of early training is for your puppy not to realise that lessons have commenced.

FIRST LESSONS
EQUIPMENT NEEDED
1. A long, light rope lead with a metal ring so that it forms its own collar, like a noose (dogs working in the shooting field or at a trial do not wear collars).
2. A plastic whistle (plastic is better than bone, as if the whistle is lost it can be replaced with another plastic one, which will have exactly the same tone).
3. You will need a number of dummies, some of which must float. At the beginning you can make your own from stuffed socks, for it is important that the dummy is not too heavy. Later on, if you find you have a hidden handicraft talent, you can make one which has a top layer of rabbit skin that has been 'cured' and so is pliant. Duck wings can also be put round a dummy, giving the first feel of retrieving feather.

GOLDEN RULES
A good time to start proper training in the spring or summer when the longer hours of daylight give more time. Never, never carry on training sessions for too long. Stop once the exercise is performed correctly, and if your puppy is struggling with a lesson, finish the session by running through something that has been taught and your puppy can do correctly. At the beginning, train where it is quiet and nobody is watching. When you have reached a certain stage, you will want to join a gundog training class, but not with your completely untrained puppy. When you are both ready, the classes are ideal for teaching your dog to work in company with lots of distractions, just like you will meet in the shooting field.

SIT ON COMMAND
When your puppy is paying attention, give the command "Sit", and at the same time place one hand gently under the pup's chin to raise the head, and with your other hand gently press the hindquarters down. Once the puppy is sitting, give plenty of praise and keep the puppy sitting for one minute, still praising. Then, let the puppy get up, choosing a release word.

SIT AND STAY
When you start to teach this exercise, only move away a stride's distance when your puppy is in the "Sit", and gradually increase the distance. However, if the puppy moves, go back and replace the puppy on the original spot. Give plenty of praise, and only move away a short distance. Change your direction; do not always go the same way, walk round your puppy, and always, at this stage, go back to your puppy. Do not call the puppy to you; the puppy must have a clear understanding of what is wanted.

Your puppy will have the instinct to retrieve, but you will need to formalise this with training.

The whistle can be introduced at an early stage, and your puppy will soon respond to it.

Always be lavish in your praise when your puppy completes an exercise successfully.

Pitcote Hooray Henry of Peredhil: Obedience trained, BOB winner, placed in Working Trials

STAYING WHILE THE DUMMY IS THROWN

You do not want your puppy to think everything thrown is to be retrieved at once. A puppy must learn steadiness. Make the puppy sit (on the lead if you wish), throw the dummy, but do not let the puppy dash off after it. Say "No", and then you go and retrieve it, once again restraining the puppy and using the command "No". Decide which dummy you will let the puppy retrieve, and then let the puppy fetch it on command. This part of the training programme can go on for quite a time – more haste less speed. Do not be tempted to try and rush this stage. Your puppy must be steady on dummies before going on to the next stage.

WALKING TO HEEL

You started this lesson with your young puppy, and you will have continued with this exercise while doing the other training. The word to use is "Heel", and if the puppy moves in front, do an about-turn so that the puppy is back in the correct position, and then repeat the "Heel" command.

The about-turn shows the puppy that you do not move on unless everybody stays in the right place, firstly on the lead, then off-lead. When your puppy is walking to heel correctly, you can extend the exercise so that when you halt, the puppy is trained to sit.

The whistle can be introduced and used instead of certain voice/word commands. The sound of a whistle travels further than your voice, it saves your voice, and it is easier to use all-round. One sharp blast equals "Sit" or "Stop", and for bringing the puppy in to the handler, use a series of short double notes. When the puppy comes in to the name, then use the name and recall whistle, and give lots of praise. When the puppy comes in at once for instant recall, you can give a tidbit, but only at the beginning. You have to be careful that, later on, when the dog is coming in with a dummy or bird, it is retrieved to hand, and not dropped in the expectation of a tidbit.

INTRODUCTION TO GUNFIRE

This must be done very carefully and gradually in the very early stages, and it should not be associated with an action, e.g. retrieving. So, when the puppy is feeding or playing quite a distance away and out of sight, get someone to fire a starting pistol periodically. The starting pistol, and later on, the gun, should be fired so that the wind is blowing away from the puppy, and thus the bang is carried away. You need to remember the opposite when throwing something for your puppy to retrieve. Make sure the wind is blowing towards the puppy, bringing the scent with it. When your puppy is completely used to the starting pistol, you can use the same principles with real gunfire. Gun-shyness is shown by absolute blind panic; nervousness of the gun is when the dog runs away a short distance, flattens the ears and cringes. However, this can be cured with skill, patience, and time.

POINTS TO WATCH FOR

Gundog training is not a race – all puppies take varying times to learn. Give short lessons and a combination of different lessons, progressing gradually. Always finish the lesson on a good note, and never let the puppy get away with rank disobedience; go back and do something that the puppy will do obediently. Do not push beyond the puppy's proven capacity at the time. When the puppy can do the exercises mentioned previously, you have reached the stage when your local gundog training club will help you to continue training, whether you are aiming for the pleasure of taking your dog out to pick up on a shooting day, or competing in Working Tests or Field Trials.

Working Tests provide an excellent outlet, after training, to use the working instincts of the Golden Retriever where it is impossible to carry on with shooting days and Field Trials. Novice Working Tests are usually composed of four or five exercises, and points are given for accurate marking, speed, delivery, and heel-keeping. Steadiness is essential. The tests will usually include a retrieve of an unseen dummy; marked retrieves over a jump and across water can be added. Dogs are tested on their stopping and taking directions. Field Trials are run as close as possible to a day's shooting, but they are designed to see the dog work and not on how many birds can be shot. Retriever Trials are usually run in two ways – by walking up or by having drives. As a trial is run on the real thing, i.e. live game, it cannot be arranged that all dogs have equal opportunities.

Chapter Eight

THE BREED STANDARD

What is the Standard of the breed? Quite simply, it is the blueprint for the perfect Golden Retriever. Who owns the Breed Standard? In the UK the copyright is owned by the Kennel Club, and in the USA it is owned by the American Kennel Club. As the Golden Retriever is indigenous to Great Britain and the breed was evolved here, this is where the original Standard was drawn up. It is, therefore, the Standard followed by countries governed by the Federation Cynologique Internationale (FCI).

Mrs Charlsworth: A pioneer of the breed and instrumental in drawing up the first Breed Standard. She is pictured with Noranby Sandy (left) and Noranby Balfour. Sandy was the first Golden Retriever to run in Field Trials and was awarded many certificates of merit. Balfour was the sire of Roy of Bentley and grandsire of Ch. Michael of Moreton.

DRAWING UP A STANDARD

In 1913 the Golden Retriever Club was founded by the first pioneer breeders, led by Mrs Winifred Maude Charlsworth. These early breeders drew up a standard of points which is still part of the present Breed Standard. The Standard was drawn up to describe the correct construction for a Golden Retriever to do the job of work it was bred for; that job was to recover game and bring it back to the handler. The Golden Retriever had to be built for pace and endurance, to carry weight and jump with it, and to have the ability to track. This perfect gundog construction described in the Standard is, therefore, used as the basis by which one dog is judged to be better than another at the dog show, thus enabling the judge to decide which dog is nearest to the 'ideal' dog of the breed as laid down in the Standard. Standards serve at least three purposes:

1. To set ideal, though attainable, goals for the breeder.
2. To guide the judge.
3. To guide the prospective purchaser who is just using 'the book' Standard.

THE BRITISH BREED STANDARD

GENERAL APPEARANCE Symmetrical, balanced, active, powerful, level mover; sound with kindly expression.

CHARACTERISTICS Biddable, intelligent and possessing natural working ability.

TEMPERAMENT Kindly, friendly and confident.

HEAD AND SKULL Balanced and well-chiselled, skull broad without coarseness; well set on neck, muzzle powerful, wide and deep. Length of foreface approximately equals length from well-defined stop to occiput. Nose preferably black.

EYES Dark brown, set well apart, dark rims.

EARS Moderate size, set on approximate level with eyes.

MOUTH Jaws strong, with a perfect, regular and complete scissor bite, i.e. upper teeth closely overlapping lower teeth and set to the jaws.

NECK Good length, clean and muscular.

FOREQUARTERS Forelegs straight with good bone, shoulders well laid back, long in blade with upper arm of equal length placing legs well under body. Elbows close fitting.

BODY Balanced, short coupled, deep through heart. Ribs deep and well sprung. Level topline.

HINDQUARTERS Loin and legs strong and muscular, good second thighs, well bent stifles. Hocks well let down, straight when viewed from rear, neither turning in nor out. Cowhocks highly undesirable.

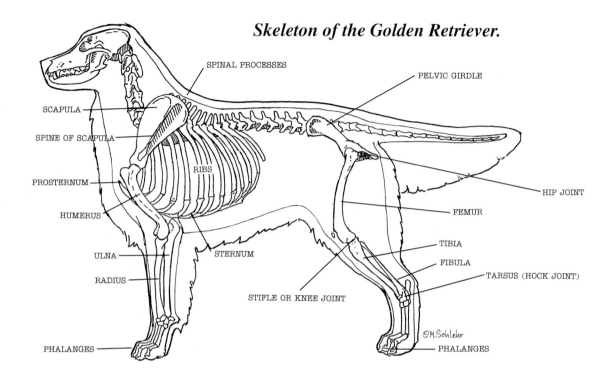

Skeleton of the Golden Retriever.

FEET Round and cat-like.

TAIL Set on and carried level with back, reaching the hocks, without curl at tip.

GAIT/MOVEMENT Powerful with good drive. Straight and true in front and rear. Stride long and free with no sign of hackney action in front.

COAT Flat or wavy with good feathering, dense water-resisting undercoat.

COLOUR Any shade of gold or cream, neither red nor mahogany. A few white hairs on chest only, permissible.

SIZE Height at withers: Dogs 56-61 cms (22-24 ins.); Bitches 51-56 cms (20-22 ins.).

FAULTS Any departure from the foregoing points should be considered a fault and the seriousness with which the fault should be regarded should be in exact proportion to its degree.

NOTE Male animals should have two apparently normal testicles fully descended into the scrotum.

Reproduced by kind permission of the English Kennel Club.

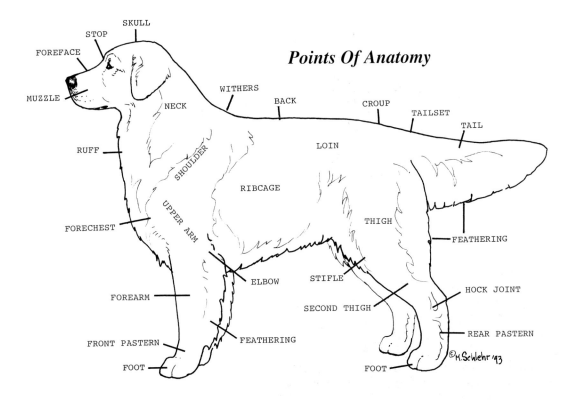

Points Of Anatomy

THE AMERICAN BREED STANDARD

GENERAL APPEARANCE

A symmetrical, powerful active dog, sound and well put together, not clumsy nor long in the leg, displaying a kindly expression and possessing a personality that is eager, alert and self-confident. Primarily a hunting dog, he should be shown in hard working condition. Overall appearance, balance, gait and purpose to be given more emphasis than any of his component parts. *Faults* – Any departure from the described ideal shall be considered faulty to the degree which it interferes with the breed's purpose or is contrary to breed character.

SIZE, PROPORTION, SUBSTANCE

Males 23-24 inches in height at withers; females 21½-22½ inches. Dogs of up to one inch above or below standard size should be proportionately penalized. Deviation in height of more than one inch from the standard shall disqualify. Length from breastbone to point of buttocks slightly greater than height at withers in ratio of 12:11. Weight for dogs 65-75 lbs; bitches 55-65 lbs.

HEAD

Broad in skull, slightly arched laterally and longitudinally without prominence of frontal bones or occipital bones. Stop well defined but not abrupt. Foreface deep and wide, nearly as long as skull.

Muzzle straight in profile, blending smoothly and strongly into skull; when viewed in profile or from above, slightly deeper and wider at stop than at tip. No heaviness in flews. Removal of whiskers is permitted but not preferred.

Eyes friendly and intelligent in expression, medium size with dark, close-fitting rim, set well apart and reasonably deep in sockets. Colour preferably dark brown, medium brown acceptable. Slant eyes and narrow, triangular eyes detract from correct expression and are to be faulted. No white or haw visible when looking straight ahead. Dogs showing function abnormality of eyelids or eyelashes (such as, but not limited to, trichiasis, entropion, ectropion or distichiasis) are to be excused from the ring.

Ears rather short with front edge attached well behind and just above the eye and falling close to cheek. When pulled forward, tip of ear should just cover the eye. Low, hound-like ear set to be faulted.

Nose Black or brownish in colour, though fading to a lighter shade in cold weather not serious. Pink nose or one seriously lacking in pigmentation to be faulted.

Teeth scissors bite, in which the outer side of the lower incisors touches inner side of the upper incisors. Undershot or overshot bite is a *disqualification*. Misalignment of teeth (irregular placement of incisors) or a level bite (incisors meet each other edge to edge) is undesirable, but not to be confused with undershot or overshot. Full dentition. Obvious gaps are serious faults.

NECK, TOPLINE, BODY

Neck medium long, merging gradually into well-laid-back shoulders, giving sturdy muscular appearance. No throatiness.

Backline strong and level from withers to slightly sloping croup, whether standing or moving. Sloping backline, roach or sway back, flat or steep croup to be faulted.

Body well balanced, short coupled, deep through chest. *Chest* between forelegs at least as wide as a man's closed hand, including thumb, with well-developed forechest. Brisket extends to elbows. *Ribs* long and well sprung but not barrel-shaped, extending well towards hindquarters. *Loin* short, muscular, wide and deep with very little tuck up. Back line strong and level from withers to slightly sloping croup whether standing or moving. Slab-sidedness, narrow chest, lack of depth in brisket, sloping back line, roach or sway back, excessive tuck-up, flat or steep croup to be faulted.

Tail well set on, thick and muscular at the base, following the natural line of the croup. Tail bones extend to, but not below, the point of the hock carried with a merry action, level with or some moderate upward curve, never curled over back or between legs.

FOREQUARTERS

Muscular, well co-ordinated with hindquarters, and capable of free movement. *Shoulder blades* long and well laid back with upper tips fairly close together at withers. *Upper arms* appear about the same length as the blades, setting the elbow back beneath the upper tip of the blades, close to the ribs without looseness. *Legs* viewed from the front, straight with good bone but not to the point of coarseness. *Pasterns* short and strong, sloping slightly with no suggestion of weakness.

Feet medium size, round and compact and well knuckled, with thick pads. Excess hair may be trimmed to show size and contour. Dewclaws on forelegs may be removed but are normally left on. Splay or hare feet to be faulted.

HINDQUARTERS

Broad and strongly muscled. Profile of croup slopes slightly; the pelvic bone slopes at a slightly greater angle (approximately 30 degrees from the horizontal). In a natural stance, the femur joins the pelvis at approximately a 90 degrees angle; *stifles* well bent; *hocks* well let down with short, strong *rear pasterns*. *Feet* as in front. *Legs* straight when viewed from rear. Cow hocks, spread hocks and sickle hocks to be faulted.

COAT

Dense and water-repellent with good undercoat. Outer coat firm and resilient, neither coarse nor silky, lying close to body; may be straight or wavy. Untrimmed natural ruff; moderate feathering on back of forelegs and on underbody; heavier feathering on front of neck, back of thighs and underside of tail. Coat on head, paws and front of legs is short and even. Excessive length, open coats and limp, soft coats are very undesirable. Feet may be trimmed and stray hairs neatened, but the natural appearance of coat or outline should not be altered by cutting or clipping.

COLOR

Rich, lustrous golden of various shades. Feathering may be lighter than rest of coat. With the exception of greying or whitening of face or body due to age, any white marking, other than a few white hairs on the chest, should be penalized according to its extent. Allowable light shadings not to be confused with white marking. Predominant body color which is extremely pale or extremely dark is undesirable. Some latitude should be given to the light puppy whose colouring shows promise of deepening with maturity. Any noticeable area of black or other off-color hair is a serious fault.

GAIT

When trotting, gait is free, smooth, powerful and well co-ordinated, showing good reach. Viewed from any position, legs turn neither in nor out, nor do feet cross or interfere with each other. As speed increases, feet tend to converge towards centre line of balance. It is recommended that dogs be shown on a loose lead to reflect true gait.

TEMPERAMENT

Friendly, reliable and trustworthy. Quarrelsomeness or hostility towards other dogs or people in normal situations, or an unwarranted show of timidity or nervousness, is not in keeping with Golden Retriever character. Such actions should be penalized according to their significance.

DISQUALIFICATIONS

Deviation in height of more than one inch from standard either way.
Undershot or overshot bite.

Approved October 13, 1981. Reformatted August 18, 1990.

Reproduced by kind permission of the American Kennel Club.

Ch. Styal Scott of Glengilde: Breed record holder with 40 CCs.   *David Dalton.*

DEFINITION OF BREED TERMS

Before I go through the Standard giving my personal interpretation, let me try to define some words that are often used when analysing character and conformation of pedigree dogs:

TYPE: Basically, 'type' is what separates one breed from another, and also that which makes a dog different in individual aspects from another dog of the same breed. True type based on function is always completely balanced.

SOUNDNESS: This means a dog has all its proper physical parts in the correct place and functioning correctly. The term is often used in reference to movement, and a dog must move correctly for its breed.

SOUND: We should use the old saying 'sound in mind and body,' and this gives the correct temperament for the breed.

QUALITY: This describes the dog that has a combination of type, soundness, temperament, breed balance, and style.

INTERPRETING THE STANDARD

GENERAL APPERANCE

This is equivalent to the first picture or impression you have of a dog when you are judging.

Everything must be in proportion, designed for a gundog to do a job of work. Theoretically, a Golden Retriever has to keep going all day over variable terrain. The dog must not be too heavy in bone, and must have the correct construction for carrying game and, if necessary, jumping while carrying it. Balance should be evident not only in neck, shoulders, ribs and length of legs, but also in the lay of the shoulders and stifle angulation. A dog that is made right will move right, so level movement should look easy and effortless, as if the dog could move all day, and if that dog was a horse, it would be comfortable to ride. There are no sharp angles, only curves, and once you have seen a number of top-class Goldens, there is no mistaking perfect balance.

TEMPERAMENT

The ability to steal into your heart is all tied up with the Golden Retriever's kindly, friendly, confident manner. Goldens are gentle with children, and never look for trouble with other dogs. They are intelligent and loyal; they are responsive – some Goldens 'grin' or 'smile' at times – and they share a great desire to please and a general air of tolerance.

The instinct to retrieve is very strong – even a baby puppy has the inborn instinct to retrieve, and gifts are brought to you from an early age. They are not, as a breed, intended to be watch dogs, but they have keen senses and they make excellent guide dogs for the blind, hearing dogs, and therapy dogs, as well as working as gundogs, competing in Obedience, and just living as part of the family.

HEAD AND SKULL

A head, according to the Standard, is essential for true breed type. It should be well-proportioned, with a broad, slightly rounded skull that is never coarse. The Golden Retriever is built to retrieve game, so a strong muzzle is essential. The muzzle should not be narrow, wedge-shaped or weak. A well-defined stop means there should be an adequate indentation between the eyes. The length of the foreface approximately equals the length from the well-defined stop to the occiput. The occiput is on top of the head – the bony protrusion – but it must not be too prominent. The nose preferably black; some become paler in winter and if this happens, the full, black pigmentation is rarely regained.

Correct head.

Weak; 'shark-faced'; snipey muzzle.

Coarse; unbalanced; loose skin.

EYES

The eyes give that lovely expression, so shape and colour are very important. They should be dark brown but not black, which spoils the expression, and light-yellow eyes also spoil that special look. Years ago, field trial trainers claimed that light-eyed dogs had better sight, but no proof was given for this statement. The shape is also important, as small eyes and large prominent eyes destroy that vital expression. We are looking for eyes of medium size, tight eyelids (loose eyelids are incorrect) and dark pigmentation round the eye-rim, and the eyes should not be set too close together, but just apart enough to appear balanced in the skull.

EARS

In profile, you see the correct position for the ears, approximately level with the eyes. Again the set of the ear can completely change the expression. They should be of moderate size. If they are too large they look very houndy. If they are too small they look as if they have been glued on.

MOUTH

A strong jaw is essential as this is a dog required to carry heavy burdens such as birds and rabbits. The teeth should be strong and set into the jaw in a scissor bite, i.e. the top teeth fitting over the bottom teeth and the surface of the lower incisors just touching the inside surface of the upper incisors. Full dentition gives the dog 42 teeth. Missing teeth (usually premolars) are penalised more severely outside the UK, where gaps are considered a serious fault. An 'even' or 'level' bite' means the teeth meet end-to-end, and this is incorrect. In an 'undershot' bite the bottom teeth project in front of the upper jaw, and an 'overshot' bite is the opposite, with the top teeth projecting well over the bottom teeth and not touching them.

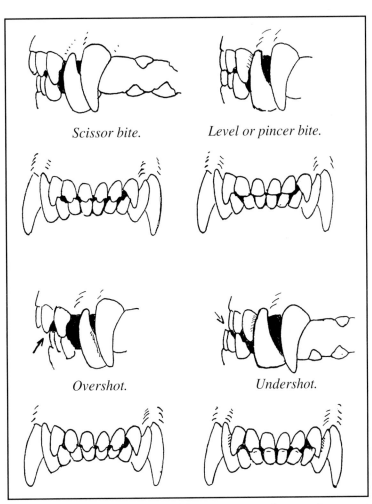

Scissor bite.   *Level or pincer bite.*

Overshot.   *Undershot.*

NECK

When you look at the Golden Retriever the neck, plus the shoulders, are among the most important constructional aspects that give the breed that essential balance. The neck must be of a good length and muscular, as this is required for carrying game over rough grounds, and for jumping and swimming while still carrying the game. The neck should merge gradually into the withers for, rather like eggs and bacon, necks and shoulders go together. The term "clean" in the British Standard equates with "no throatiness" in the American Standard, meaning there should be no loose skin.

FOREQUARTERS

Front legs should be straight, and that gives you tight, not loose, elbows. Bone should be ample,

Good front.

Too straight, no forechest.

Overdone, 'loaded shoulders, weak pasterns.

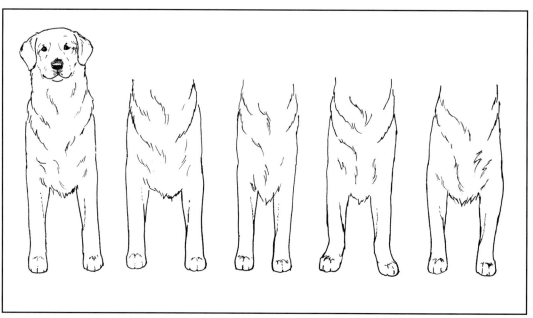

Correct forequarters.

Too wide

Too narrow.

'East-west' or 'French' chest.

Out at elbows.

but not too heavily-boned which leads to coarseness – a Golden Retriever should not have the bone of a Newfoundland. This is one point of the Standard in which the pure show and pure field lines have separated because of their respective requirements. The front pasterns should be strong with not too much slope, leading into round cat-like, well-knuckled feet. This, again, is a requirement based on the type of land the Golden was bred to work on. The feet act as shock-absorbers; splayed, flat feet at a 'Charlie Chaplin' angle are incorrect.

The shoulders must be so designed as to follow on and place the legs well under the body, which means about a 90 degree angle between the shoulder blade (scapula) and the upper arm (humerus). The shoulder blade and upper arm are roughly the same in length. The shoulder blade must be well laid back. In order for front movement to be correct, the assembly must work as a whole.

BODY

Again, the emphasis is on balance. Everything must be in proportion, and the body should be short coupled. However, 'short' does not become a virtue if it stems from upright, steep shoulders. The body should have more length than height, so that the ribs extend well back. Too much cobbiness is incorrect, just as is too much length, which often leads to weak backs.

A working blueprint is for ribs to be well-sprung, giving plenty of heart room. A ribcage that is too round can spoil the front movement, making the dog out at elbow or toe in. If the brisket lacks depth the dog can look leggy. The correct, level topline comes from the correct balance of body and ribs. The correct set-on of tail helps to make that level topline, and the tail is carried level with back when the dog is moving. In length, the tail should reach the hock joint.

The loin must be short and muscular – imbalance comes from length of the loin. The ribs can be felt, but the eye will tell you if they are too flat or too rounded, and this is where too much weight can ruin the balance. If the brisket is too deep, the dog will appear short on the leg and thick all

Correct level topline.

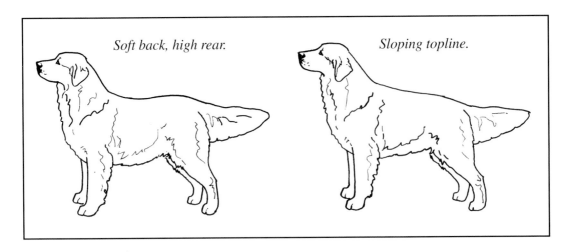

Soft back, high rear.   *Sloping topline.*

through. A tail carried 'gaily' or too high, is an obvious fault when a dog is moving in profile, but a dog can also be faulted for carrying the tail too low so that it seems to be falling off the croup. It is not allowed for the tail to curl at the tip, and this is usually trimmed off.

HINDQUARTERS

The Golden Retriever needs hindquarters that will be powerful and will provide the thrust that will keep the dog moving and working all day. Again, that perfect balance is gained with proper angulation behind. As you watch the dog move away in a straight line, you see that the hocks provide the drive, and they should not turn out or in (the hock is the joint between the second thigh and the pastern). The hock should be moderately low; it is a fault is if the hocks incline towards each other, turning inwards, which is known as cow-hocks. The Standard asks for well-bent stifles. A dog with straight stifles will never move with a smooth, free-striding action.

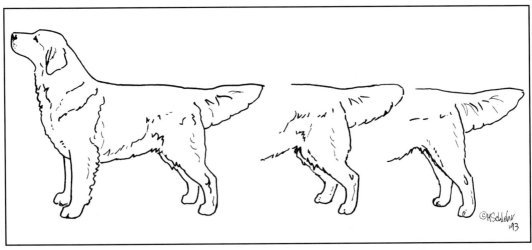

Good angulation.   *Too bent:*   *Too straight.*
                     'sickle-hocked'.

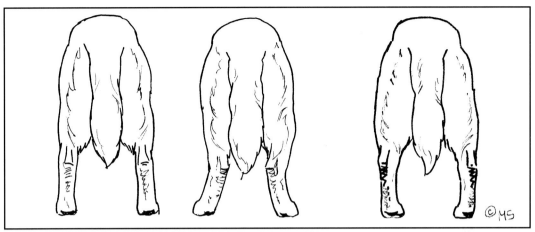

Good rear.   *Cow-hocked.*   *Bowed rear.*

MOVEMENT

Golden Retrievers should be made so that they cover the ground smoothly, without apparent effort. Over-angulated stifles usually lead to weakness behind. The movement is straight and true in front, so correct construction should give correct movement. The stride should be long and free, coming from correct shoulders, with no high-stepping or hackney action. This would be a useless action for a dog required to work all day over different types of terrain – it would be such a waste of energy. If the dog is constructed with steep shoulders and a steep rear, the dog will move with short steps.

COAT

This should be flat or wavy, never curly, with ample feathering. It should be dense with a water-resisting undercoat. This means the top hairs are longer and the undercoat is dense to make a waterproof texture, which is especially for the working dog.

COLOUR

This is one of the most controversial features – and it is a subject many people feel strongly about. The British Standard allows any shade of gold or cream, neither red nor mahogany. The American Standard states: "Rich, lustrous golden of various shades... Predominant body colour which is either extremely pale or extremely dark is undesirable." There is, therefore, a definite split between the two countries, as the cream colour is popular among British Golden Retrievers.

When the British Standard was first compiled in the early 1900s, cream was not included as a permitted colour, but in 1936 the Standard was altered to allow "cream – any shade of gold or cream." Mrs Charlsworth, probably the most influential figure in the early Show Trial years of the Golden Retriever from 1910 onwards, wrote in *The Book of the Golden Retriever* (published 1933): "Those of us who drew up the Standard of Points in the early days realised that the foundation colour of the original Guisachan strain was cream and knew the difficulty, if not the impossibility, of completely eradicating this colour. I thought then, as I do now, that a mistake was made in forbidding cream colour, but my views were in the minority."

The British and American Standards both allow a range of goldens, and one shade of the range is no better than the other. Judges who write in critiques "correct colour" are showing they do not understand plain English. Mrs Charlsworth writes: "ripe cornfields of wheat, oats and barley" are to be found in the range. Years ago, I was told a new golden guinea should match the Golden Retriever coat – but there are not many of these around nowadays! I have given Challenge Certificates to animals within the whole range allowed by the Standard. You must never judge on colour as long as it is within the range, that is all you have to worry about.

WEIGHT

The British Standard no longer has an ideal weight in the Standard. This has been discarded, but there is an interesting story which relates to the original weight stipulations. When Golden Retriever enthusiasts in North America wanted to import and start the breed there, they wanted to know what was considered the ideal height and weight. As a result, top dogs in the UK were weighed and measured. The American Standard now states: "Weight for dogs 65-75 pounds; bitches 55-65 pounds."As far as weight is concerned, you must learn to use your own eye, for the dog constructed for work must not be overweight. The ribs must be nicely covered, you must not be able to see the ribs or 'pin bones' on the quarters, and it is important to remember that dogs and bitches will not stay at the ideal weight but will tend to go a little over or under. This often occurs when dogs are near bitches in season or being used at stud; bitches may vary according to their seasonal cycle, and puppies will obviously change at different stages of their growth.

HEIGHT

There is a bigger range of height allowed in the British Standard: "Dogs 56-61 cms (22-24 inches), bitches 51-56 cms (20-22 inches)" compared with the American Standard: "Males 23-24 inches in height at withers; females $21_{1/2}$–$22_{1/2}$ inches." Height is the most difficult thing to assess visually. The balance of the dog's construction can make it difficult, and, remember, perfect balance always tends to make a dog look smaller. Mark the height limits on an outside wall, make a guess, and then check the dogs against it. When I am judging a new breed I always measure what the height allowance is against my leg, and then, in the ring when I am going over the animal, I check against my leg. Often you hear people saying that an animal (usually a bitch) is too small, yet when measured she will turn out to be within the Standard.

FAULTS

Before discussing this heading, let me emphasise that the perfect dog has never been born. Every dog has faults, and in Britain the problem is highlighted by the all-embracing clause: "Any departure from the foregoing points should be considered a fault and the seriousness with which the fault should be regarded should be in exact proportion to its degree." This seems like passing the buck, leaving the judge to decide, for example, whether light eyes are a more serious fault than a gay tail. However, there are some faults – for example, those that affect movement, teeth and jaw, or construction, and any other faults that would prevent the dog doing the job it was initially bred for – which must be considered serious. The American Standard states: "Any departure from the described ideal shall be considered faulty to the degree which it interferes with the breed's purpose or is contrary to breed character", which gives a far clearer indication what is intended.

   The judge's job is to assess how closely a dog fits the Standard. But, be warned: never fall into the trap of fault-judging, only noticing the faults and not the virtues, as you could end up with the mediocre. Over the years, I have seen top awards go to dogs with many faults, but on the day, the judge obviously decided that their virtues outweighed their faults.

Line drawings by Marcia Schelehr.

Chapter Nine

THE SHOW RING

If you want to show your Golden Retriever, this could be the start of a whole new way of life. You may start off with one dog of show quality, attending the occasional show, but if you get bitten by the show-going bug, you will soon have few spare weekends left in your calendar! Dog shows are licensed by the national Kennel Club, and there are different types of shows available, depending on the level of competition.

BRITISH SHOWS

MATCHES: These are held between dog clubs, using dog against dog in a knock-out system. No Challenge Certificate winners.

Westley Glenn of Highguild waiting to go into the ring. Showing should be fun for both dog and handler.

David Dalton

EXEMPTION SHOWS: Registered at the Kennel Club, unregistered dogs are eligible to enter and there are no more than four pedigree classes. The other classes are Novelty Classes, e.g. 'dog with the longest eye-lashes'.

PRIMARY SHOW: Entry is limited to members of the Show Society classes for puppies and novice dogs, thus no Challenge Certificate winners.

LIMITED AND SANCTION SHOWS: Entry is limited to members of the Show Society. No winners of Challenge Certificates can be shown.

OPEN SHOWS: These are open to all exhibitors and a Breed Club can hold such a Show for one breed. No Challenge Certificates awarded.

CHAMPIONSHIP SHOWS: These are are open to all breeds or named Breed Clubs and Kennel Club Challenge Certificates are offered. Three such Challenge Certificates allows a dog to be called a Show Champion in Gundogs. One of the Challenge Certificates has to be won when the animal is over 12 months.

AMERICAN SHOWS

MATCHES: The local All Breed and Specialty Clubs will probably hold one or two Matches a year. These are advertised in the canine press, giving details of breeds, classes and judges. Entries are made on the morning of the show. They are often used as a training ground for people who are aspiring to judge at Championship show level. Classes usually range from Puppy through Novice to Open. Champions are not eligible to compete in Matches.

CHAMPIONSHIP SHOWS: These can be All Breed, Group or Breed shows. They are advertised in the canine press, and premiums are sent to all intending exhibitors. After the closing date for entries, passes, catalog numbers and schedules are sent to exhibitors. Points are awarded towards the Championship title by a judge who is approved by the Kennel Club. A total of fifteen points under three different judges must be gained for a dog to become a Champion, including two 'majors' under separate judges (3, 4, or 5 point wins).

The size of the major is decided by the number of dogs entered at a show. The scale of Championship points is decided by the American Kennel Club, and this is calculated on the average number of Golden Retrievers shown in various regions of the USA.

SPECIALTIES: These are held annually or bi-annually by the club concerned, usually attracting large entries. Again, Championship points are awarded. The judge is normally someone held in high esteem by breeders and exhibitors, and sometimes an overseas judge receives an invitation to judge.

RING TRAINING

You will have to wait until your Golden Retriever is six months of age before you can enter for a show, but there is plenty of work to do beforehand. Ring training classes are run by many breed clubs, and this is a very useful place for you and your puppy to learn what is required in the show ring. Once the vaccination programme has been completed, you can take your puppy to a ring

The American style: Ch. Asterling's Tahiti Sweetie basking in the glory at a National Specialty.

J. Luria.

training (ringcraft) class. To begin with, you can just sit and watch, and your puppy will get used to being with other dogs. At around four months of age, your puppy will be ready to take part.

The aim of ring training is to go through all the show ring procedures, so both handler and dog become accustomed to the routine. The puppy will get used to being examined by a stranger, and you will learn how to stand your dog and to move in the correct fashion. It is far better to learn in this non-competitive atmosphere rather than at a show itself. Matches are sometimes held, and this will give you even more experience. I am a great believer in ring training. I find nothing clever in the exhibitor who turns up at a show, with a wild, panicking puppy, saying proudly: "He's never been on a lead before today." This is not fair to the puppy, or to the other exhibitors in the class. My local class has many famous breeders who attend with their puppies. Champion Pekingese, Champion Miniature Schnauzers, and Show Champion Golden Retrievers and Clumber Spaniels have all first trod the mat at Macclesfield, and, in the less stressed atmosphere of a club, everybody will be prepared help a newcomer.

The art of handling your dog in the show ring is to show off all the good points and disguise any faults. The judge will go over each dog in turn, and this involves laying on of hands to assess construction, opening the mouth to check for correct dentition, feeling the coat texture, checking males are entire, and then watching the handler move the dog, usually in a triangle and then straight up and down. 'Moving' means getting your dog to trot at your side, freely on a loose lead, and the judge will stand and watch your dog very closely.

Golden Retrievers can be shown in two ways – free standing or stacked. A free standing pose entails the dog walking into position so the feet are in the correct place, and the dog should look up at you, gently wagging the tail. A necessary part of this style is a pocketful of tidbits, which are

Sh.Ch. Tasvane
Charles Henry:
Free-standing.

used to hold the dog's attention. A stacked pose means that you keep your hand under the dog's chin, place the fore feet and hind feet in position, and the hold the tail at the tip out so that it carries on the line of the topline. Both poses are held when the judge is looking at the dog, and then relaxed while you are waiting. Both are attractive when done correctly. Nothing quite beats the free standing, looking up at you with interested expression, gently waving tail, but it takes a lot of practice and must be done correctly – often people combine the two styles.

Start off by thinking of a command word which the dog will start to associate with an instruction. Place the feet, then say "Stand" followed by the dog's name. If the dog stands until you change the action, give lots of praise and a tidbit. Do not bore the puppy by practising for too long. A ten-minute session a day, plus one visit per week to ring training class is sufficient. When you are putting your hand under the chin there is a part of the bone that your fingers slip into; do not clutch the muzzle so that your fingers show.

Many years ago I had an English Setter who was a Show Champion with many CC to his credit, and he was slightly throaty – I often find this goes with the correct, square muzzle. Setters are not shown free standing, and I was adept at stacking him, with throat neatly tucked in. However, on one occasion we were in a Stakes Class at a Championship Show, and the judge, a famous all-

Ch. Standfast Angus:
Stacked.

rounder pulled us out first. He went to the table to get his judging book, but he turned round just as I relaxed the pose, and decided my dog had too much throat which he had not seen before, and I went down to second. The lesson learned was never relax while you are in the class – even if you think you have won.

ENTERING A SHOW
You have been going to ring training classes, and feel you want to go one step further and enter a show. When you get your show schedule, you will find there are many different classes, and you must decide which to enter. My advice is do not attempt too many. At first, restrict yourself to the age-related classes, and gradually work up the scale as you win your way out of the classes. Do not enter your two-year-old Golden Retriever at a first Championship Show in every class right up to Open. It can be a waste of your entry fee.

PREPARING YOUR DOG
Your Golden Retriever should always be kept in top-class condition, but before a show a dog will need to go through a special grooming/trimming routine so that you have every chance of success.

Gaiting: The Golden Retriever should be moved on a loose lead, trotting at your side.

David Dalton.

BATHING

If you are showing your Golden Retriever you will need bathing facilities you can use all the year round. You can buy a bath and have it plumbed into a utility room, not at floor level, but at a higher level so that you do not need to bend. It is also useful to have steps so that you do not need to lift the dog in. I have also seen a shower room adapted with a central grid and hand-held shower system on the wall, so it was just a case of walking the dog in for the bath. Hand-held showers, fitted with a temperature mixer, are the best method of wetting a dog, but do check the water is not too hot or too cold – test it on your hand first.

I always use a good-quality dog shampoo as they are designed especially for dog hair. I finish off with a cream rinse that is specially formulated for dogs. Make sure you have rinsed all the shampoo out of the dog's coat, otherwise the coat appears dull. Towel well before the dog is allowed out of the bath or shower, then there will not be so much water to shake off – and you will remain reasonably dry!

The next step is to dry the coat thoroughly. It is easiest to do this on the grooming table, using a hair-dryer, and combing as the coat dries. You can use the domestic type of hair-dryer or you can buy one of the powerful dryers used in the dog salons. Whatever type you use, it is essential to keep combing in order that the coat dries flat. You can also make a coat out of towelling. Comb the hair flat, and then put the towelling coat on and leave till dry. If your dog seems frightened of the hair-dryer and refuses to stand still, then you will have to towel dry and keep on combing. If your Golden has the correct type of coat it is going to take a long time to dry, and there is nothing worse than letting a dog go to bed when slightly damp, as by the next morning a lot of the coat will be lying the wrong way. Goldens should not be washed the night before a show. If you bath your dog a couple of days before the show, this gives a chance for the coat to get back its lovely gloss. You can buy dry-foam shampoos that act by cleaning without water. This can be useful in an emergency, especially if something goes wrong at the show. I once had a bitch who, on the way in across the car park, sniffed under an exhaust pipe and had an oily blob right on top of her head. Fortunately, the dry-foam shampoo cleaned it off beautifully. However, this type of shampoo is no substitute for washing your dog two days before the show. There are so many coat preparations you can buy nowadays, but you will soon find out what is the best for your dog.

TRIMMING
A show Golden Retriever may be trimmed to enhance the good points and show the correct outline. You cannot trim to alter the dog's construction, but trimming will maximise the best that is there. I always trim and then wash the dog because, for me, trimming looks less obvious if it is done that way. The word 'obvious' is a very important – trimming must never look obvious; you are gilding the lily, not pulling all the petals off! Even if you do not intend to show your dog it is a good idea to learn how to trim the feet, as this will limit the amount of mud and dirt brought into the house.

TRIMMING EQUIPMENT
Thinning scissors (scissors with serrated edges)
Straight-edged scissors
Nail-cutters (guillotine type are easy to use)
Metal comb
Slika brush
Bristle brush
Hound glove
Magnet stripping knife
Comb (with very fine teeth).

HOW TO TRIM
The best way to learn how to trim is to watch an experienced handler at work. Many breed clubs have trimming sessions as part of their social programme, and if it is a hands-on session you can actually get the 'feel' of trimming under the guidance of an expert. Your puppy's breeder may offer to start you off, and it is easier to start with a youngster who will not have as much coat as an adult.

If you are trimming an adult with a lot of coat, do not make the mistake of starting the night before the show and expect it to be done in five minutes. Begin your trimming two or three weeks before the show and do an half-hour session each week, culminating in the final tidy-up before you wash the dog. There are some important points to remember when trimming your Golden Retriever:

1. It is better to take off too little hair when first trimming rather than too much – you cannot glue it on again!
2. Always use your thinning scissors and then comb through, to get the effect of what you have removed.
3. Never cut across the hair.

THE ART OF TRIMMING
Demonstrated by
Bernard Bargh.
Photographs by
David Dalton.

Start off by trimming
the neck and chest.

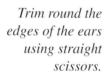

Trim round the
edges of the ears
using straight
scissors.

Merge the neck, trimming into the shoulders.

The tail should have longer hair at the base, gradually becoming shorter until it is rounded off at the tip.

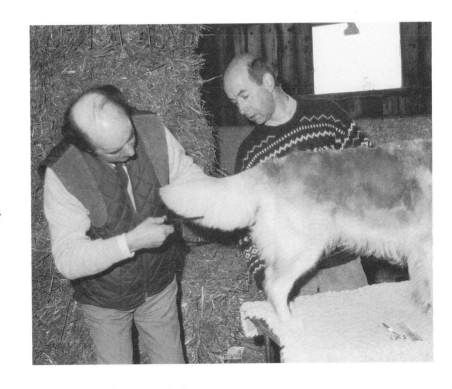

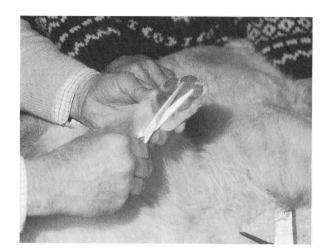

Trim away excess fur around the pads.

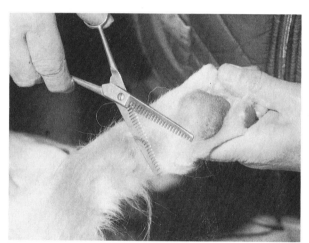

Neaten the straggly feathering on the edge of the pastern.

Use the thinning scissors to remove excess hair from the hock.

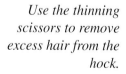
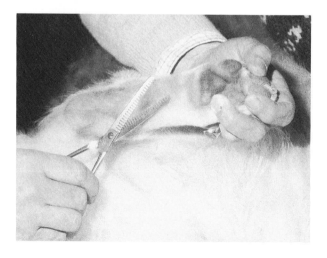

4. Always use an upward movement and push the scissors underneath the top layer.
5. Keep combing throughout the trimming session.

Start off by trimming the neck and chest and carry on until you have done the whole chest, not forgetting the hair underneath the ears and also the hair on top and around the ear flap. Trim around the edges of the ears with the straight scissors, and do be careful when trimming under the ears as there is a double fold which you can catch with the scissors. Merge the neck trimming into the shoulders, and then let the dog rest.

For the next trimming session, concentrate on the tail. It is a good idea to have a look at pictures of Golden Retrievers with trimmed tails. The shape you are aiming for is longer hair at the base, gradually becoming shorter until it is rounded off at the tip. When the judge measures the tail it will be by seeing if the tip reaches the top of the hock. Hold the tail out by the tip, take the straight scissors and trim from the tip to the root in an arc, leaving the hair at its longest point at about four to five inches. Let the hair fall into place, comb, and you may need to trim again to tidy up.

Next, look at the trouser feathering, Does it need to be tidied? This should be done by sticking up pieces of hair and pulling against the magnet stripper. The stripper can also be used on the top of the ears, or for any long guard hairs that do not lie flat. However, do be careful, the magnet trimmer is as sharp as a razor. You will need to trim off any extra long thin hairs below the body line of feathering, and you will find the fine-toothed comb is ideal for bringing out the coat when the dog is starting to cast.

When you start work on the feet, you will find it easier if your dog is lying down. Pull the excess long hair up between the toes, and cut down with the straight scissors, Then check under the foot, around the pads, and trim away excess fur. Neaten the straggly feathering on the edge of the pastern, and do the same with the excess hair from hock to foot, using the thinning scissors. Remember to trim and then comb.

If the nails are long they will need cutting. You must be very careful not cut the quick, the living part of the nail. If you cut this it will bleed profusely and cause the dog a lot of pain, which may well be remembered next time you try to do the job. If the nail is light-coloured you can see the quick and gauge accordingly, but if the nails are dark, you will need to be extra careful. You will need to buy a special nail cutter for the dog's nails, and the guillotine type is very good and obtainable from most pet stores.

One final thing to remember, always keep your grooming tools in good condition. The scissors will need sharpening, and when buying scissors, always get the best – it is an economy in the long run.

THE SHOW BAG
You need to take certain things to a show for the dog, and it is a good idea to take them in a special bag. You need a rug for the dog to lie on. This is particularly important in the UK when shows are benched. In this instance you will also need a benching chain and a collar to fit the bench chain on to – never a choke-chain which can cause a terrible accident. You will need a bottle filled with water, a drinking bowl, dog food if you are going to miss the time you normally feed your dog, and therefore a bowl for the food.

You will need a brush and comb, and your straight and thinning scissors, in case your dog needs a last-minute tidy up. I also find one of the brands of liquid anti-static spray is useful to have, in case the journey has caused the coat to become very ruffled, plus a can of dry-foam shampoo, so you are prepared for all eventualities. There are many kinds of show leads. I find the best is a long

Valerie Foss (right) with Sh. Ch.Westley Simone, winner of twelve CCs.

David Dalton.

strip with a ring at one end. They come in all kinds of material, nylon, fine leather, etc. You pays your money and takes your choice – the stands at shows have hundreds to choose from. Most seasoned show dogs know that something different is happening when you get out the show lead! Choose your slip collar with care, and if it is leather keep it well cleaned so that it is soft and pliable. I would suggest you take coffee and food for yourself. Finally, choose your own clothes with care, so you are smart but comfortable. You must have shoes that you can move well in all day and, if it is an outside venue, make sure you have some waterproof gear, just in case.

THE DAY OF THE SHOW
Leave plenty of time for your journey, particularly when you are in the puppy classes as these are the first ones to be judged. When you arrive at the show, exercise your dog, making sure you dispose of any mess. In the UK dogs have to get used to being benched, and you should get your dog used to this experience, so that the dog will settle if left unattended for short periods.

Check where your ring is, and give your dog a last minute grooming. If you are not in the first class, you can watch the judge to see how the class is being conducted, and to note the patterns for movement. Then you can have a quick practice in a quiet spot of the venue and be ready to go in when the steward calls your class. When you are in the ring you are there to show your dog; chatting to ringsiders can wait till afterwards. Watch how other people show their dogs, as this might give you some pointers to improve your own performance.

BECOMING A JUDGE

BRITAIN
Like so many other 'sports', dog shows originated in the UK; the first, properly organised dog

show was held in 1859 and was limited to Pointers and Setters. The Kennel Club, the organising body for all aspects of dogs was founded in 1873, and as a result of this historical background, and the large number of dogs in Britain,the UK's system of appointing judges is different to every other country in the world. In the UK there are no formal qualifications required for judging; you wait to be asked, and then take it from there. It often seems very much a case of 'learning by discovery'. Judges mostly start out as breed or specialist judges, as I did. I first awarded Challenge Certificates in Golden Retrievers at Manchester 1966, and you either stay with just the one breed, or graduate to do other breeds as well. I now judge the whole of the Gundog Group, and award Challenge Certificates for all breeds within this Group.

AMERICA

In the USA a prospective judge must have ten years experience in breeding and exhibiting; an applicant must have bred and raised four litters of any one breed, and produced two Champions from these litters. The applicant must have stewarding experience and must have judged at AKC sanctioned Matches, Sweepstakes or Futurities. The applicant who proceeds to the next stage must pass an examination on AKC rules, policies and judging procedures; pass a written test on the Breed Standard for each of the breeds applied for, and then must be interviewed in order to demonstrate breed knowledge and qualifications. Both in America and on the Continent aspiring judges go through a period where they are watched by a representative of their Kennel Club, and, depending on the representative's reports and the results of written exams, it is decided whether the applicant is ready and suitable to judge.

THE JUDGE'S ROLE

What knowledge does a judge need? You need a thorough knowledge of the anatomy of the dog, and the Breed Standard of the Golden Retriever must be understood in depth. Obviously, everybody sees things in a slightly different way, attaching more or less importance to particular virtues or faults. This is as it should be, otherwise the same animals would always win.

However, there are certain breed points which are not open to individual interpretation. Incorrect shoulders are always wrong, dipping toplines still dip, light eyes do not darken radically, eyes that are the wrong shape do not alter, fronts that look like Chippendale chairs stay that way, coarse heads stay coarse, and straight stifles do not acquire the correct bend. Of course, a judge puts up animals with faults; the perfect dog has not been born. The aim is to find the best specimen of the breed entered under you, on that particular day. Do not write a critique failing to mention an obvious fault in a dog you have put up – you cannot pretend the fault was not in evidence on the day you were judging.

A judge should be totally unbiased, completely impartial and sufficiently clear-minded to judge what is seen on that day only. A judge should have the conviction and confidence to do what they want. Good judging is a calm evaluation of good and bad points, and a clear appreciation of the Standard, which is the blueprint by which all judges should work. One further thing to remember is that no-one has the monopoly on owning or breeding good stock – others breed good animals too; you must always judge the dogs and not their breeding.

The well-known Best in Show judge, Tom Horner, wrote in his book *Take Them Round Please*: "Judging is both an art and a science. It is an art because the decisions with which a judge is constantly faced are very often based on considerations of an intangible nature that cannot be recognised and assessed without some artistic sense. Such things as type, quality, expression and balance cannot be described adequately in exact terms, they have to be recognised intuitively. It is

Good judging is a calm evaluation of good and bad points, and a clear appreciation of the Breed Standard.

also a science because without a sound knowledge of a dog's points and anatomy, a judge cannot make a proper assessment of it, whether it is in standing or in motion. Judging should be carried out positively, i.e. the judge should look for the dogs with the most good points, not the ones with the least wrong with them – that is fault judging and is full of dangers. Sometimes the dog with the least faults is the one equally without positive virtues. Type, substance, balance, the correct conformation for its breed, sound movement and good temperament. These are the essentials."

IN THE RING
So what does the judge do, physically, as well as mentally? The class is in the ring, and the judge will have a first look as the dogs and handlers as they line up. The judge may then send the dogs round the ring once so that he/she has a chance to view the dogs moving in profile. Getting the dog moving also helps to settle the class. Each dog then comes out individually and is examined by the judge.

Most judges will start by looking at the head, checking the mouth, then moving down the neck to the point of shoulder, checking that the elbows fit properly. The judge will look for those correct tight feet, look and feel for the correct shape of ribs, checking for a nice deep brisket, short couplings, a correctly set-on tail of the right length. Muscles on the second thigh will be checked and the coat and undercoat will be assessed. A male must have two testicles.

The judge then stands back and views the overall picture, and then asks to see the dog moving in triangle and up and down, so that all aspects of the movement can be seen. The judge then uses the same procedure on each dog until they have all been examined. Then the whole class stand in line, posing their dogs. Entries are usually very large in Golden Retriever classes, and so the judge will walk around pulling out a selection, before awarding final placings.

Always congratulate the winner, no matter how disappointed you may feel. I remember talking to Rene Parsons of the famous Torrdale Golden Retrievers, and she said: "It is the easiest thing in the world to be a winner, but it takes a lot more character to be a good loser, and in any case, at the next show the positions can be reversed."

Chapter Ten

PRINCIPLES OF BREEDING

BECOMING A BREEDER

Many people become breeders and exhibitors by chance, and like most things people do, some seem to learn quickly, and many who start off well, never progress as rapidly as anticipated. When you decide to become a breeder, you must start off by taking advice, but then you must learn to think for yourself. You must study your breed, look at old photographs, learn anatomy, and learn to understand the Breed Standard.

Of course, at the beginning you are a pupil with everything to learn, but do not stay at this stage by refusing to open your mind to all strains and ideas on the breed. Do not perpetuate the myth that beginners will never progress, and only the big breeders win the prizes. Winning prizes is not about personalities, it is about who has the better dog, and probably the hardest lesson the novice has to learn is not to look at your dog through rose-tinted spectacles. See the faults in your dog, and work out how you hope to breed them out. You must strive for perfection, and never fall into the trap of being 'kennel blind'. You must be ready to listen and learn all the time.

Do not think you must always use a Champion, hoping that puppies with a Champion sire will be easier to sell, and then compounding the error by using the Champion who is doing the most winning. Only use a Champion dog that ties in with your bitch's pedigree, and who seems to have given a lot when mated to bitches of similar breeding. It is important to bear in mind that just because a dog becomes a Champion, it does not necessarily mean it is a good dog.

One problem that seems universal to all breeders is getting over-stocked. The first dog does not turn out as you would wish but, naturally, has become part of the family. The puppies kept (two at a time) do not make the grade. Then you acquire a stud dog to save money on stud fees and travelling expenses. In no time at all, you have too many dogs, and this becomes a downward spiral because you have collected too many mediocre specimens, your neighbours are starting to complain about the noise, and your family is becoming anti-show and anti-breeding – and your kennel is grinding to a halt.

Breeding carries with it a great responsibility. You have brought a litter of puppies into the world, and your involvement does not always end when they are sold at eight weeks. You must be prepared to take back a dog of your own breeding at any stage, and find new homes, if the occasion arises.

You must also be available to give advice to your puppy customers. Unfortunately, the Golden Retriever rescue organisations are left to cope with the results of uncaring and unknowledgeable breeders, who mistakenly think breeding pedigree dogs is a method of making money. Therefore, before you decide to breed a litter of puppies, whether your intention is just to breed one litter

Five Westley title-holders: The mark of a successful kennel is to consistently produce top-quality dogs of similar type.

David Dalton.

from your pet bitch, or you are trying to found a family strain under your own prefix, there are certain criteria that must be followed:

HEALTHY STOCK: You will only breed from animals with eye certificates and scored hips, and, likewise, you will expect the same from the dogs you use.

ACCOMMODATION: You have the space to house the bitch when whelping, and the facilities to cope with a litter for the first three to four weeks of puppyhood, and then the different accommodation that will be needed for the next four weeks.

TIME: Do you have you the time for whelping your bitch? You cannot go out to work and leave the bitch on her own when she is due to whelp. Rearing puppies is time-consuming – when they are weaned they will need five feeds a day!

MONEY: You will certainly not get rich breeding a litter, but more importantly, you will have to outlay a fair amount of money before you see any return. You will have to pay the stud fee of a good dog and provide top-quality food for the bitch and her puppies. If veterinary attention is required at any stage, you will have more bills to pay.

FINDING HOMES: Do you have a suitable list of purchasers for your puppies? If any of these homes falls through, do you have the facilities to keep puppies beyond eight weeks, remembering that the older the puppies become, the harder they are to sell?

If you are confident that you can cope with the full responsibility of becoming a breeder, it is time to start planning your litter.

ESTABLISHING A STRAIN

The bitch who is going to be the 'lynch-pin' of your line must be a typical Golden Retriever, conforming as closely to the Breed Standard as possible. Ideally, she should be from generations of stock with clear eye certificates and good hip scores. The bitch's temperament must be typical – kindly, friendly and confident.

You will probably start with a puppy, and while she is growing up you should learn as much as possible about genetics, i.e. the study of genes, the unique individual patterns each animal carries in the cells of their bodies. From the moment of conception, genes determine what an animal will look like, and they will also influence how that animal will behave. Genes are carried in the body on strings known as chromosomes. They vary in number according to different species – dogs have 39 pairs of chromosomes. All inheritance depends upon chromosomes: each dog inherits half its genes from the sire and half from the dam, but the result of this does not produce the intermediate or middle way. A coarse-skulled dog and a fine-skulled bitch will not produce medium-skulled progeny. Not all genes are equal, there are dominant and recessive genes. Dominant genes show in the dog or bitch, recessive genes are there but hidden, and only show when a mating takes place with a dog or bitch which also carries the gene as a recessive.

The following three methods are used to establish a strain.

IN-BREEDING

This is usually described with a "Do Not Use" warning for the novice breeder. It involves mating together animals who are very closely related, e.g. father to daughter, mother to son, brother to sister. You are not introducing any fresh blood, with the result that you are bringing out hidden faults as well as fixing the virtues. In-breeding has no favourites, it intensifies the bad as well as the good. In order to use this method successfully, you need a great knowledge of the animals and those in their pedigrees, but this method does not seem to be used as much these days. Some famous breeders had permutations which they liked very much – a bitch to her nephew, a bitch to her litter brother's best son; half-brother and sister was favoured, as was putting a bitch back to her grandfather or uncle, but full brother and sister matings were not liked. Of course, if these matings are to be attempted, the dogs must be of the highest quality.

In the early history of Golden Retrievers we have many examples of in-breeding. The highly influential Sh. Ch. Noranby Dandelion (b.1913) was the result of a mating between Ingestre Dred and Ingestre Luna, a full brother and sister. Ch. Hazelgilt (b.1934), much admired for brains and beauty was the result of a father to daughter mating (Gilder – Daleside Snipe), and although mated to few bitches he proved influential. Ch. Torrdale Happy Lad, an influential sire (b.1945) was the result of grandson, Torrdale Sandy Boy, mated to grandmother, Ch. Dukeries Dancing Lady. One of Mrs Minter's beautiful early bitches, Ch. Charming of Stenbury (b.1946) was the result of a half-brother and sister (Torrdale Don Juan – Laughter of Stenbury), with a further connection in that the dams of Don Juan and Laughter were sisters. The present UK top CC winner, Ch. Styal Scott of Glengilde, is a half-brother and sister mating (Ch. Nortonwood Faunus – Ch. Styal Susila) both by Ch. Camrose Cabus Christopher, the all-time top sire.

LINE-BREEDING

This involves mating your bitch to a dog of the same family. You gather up the lines which lead back in three or four generations to a very good dog or bitch – your pedigree will go back to this dog or bitch five or six times in five generations. This method can be very successful, but the dog or bitch you are line-breeding to must have been outstanding. The danger lies in the fact that if you only know of the dog by reputation, and not personally. If you look into the pedigrees of the great breeders in Golden Retrievers, you will see their strains are line-bred into the strain itself.

Elma Stonex (Dorcas) is known today as the greatest breed historian, but when she was breeding and showing she was a brilliant breeder. After the Second World War, she helped to set the breed back on to the correct tracks. Her foundation bitch, Sally of Perrott, won one CC and, from her photograph, was a very typical bitch. She was the result of a half-brother and sister mating (Ch. Haulstone Marker – Noranby Daphne) both by a great sire of that time, Ch. Michael of Moreton, and with many similar lines in their dams' pedigrees. Regarding Michael's influence on his progeny, Elma Stonex said: "Good heads and shoulders, quarters and activity, good workers, maybe some a bit long cast". Sally, who is probably in most pedigrees today, was nine months old when Elma Stonex bought her. Her dam was a winning working litter sister to a famous Champion of Mrs Charlsworth's great Noranby strain; Sally was the top price at £20.

By her choice of sires, Elma Stonex showed her skill. When Sally was mated to Ch. Davie of Yelme, she produced the great sire, Dorcas Bruin, 'a war baby' – which is why he never gained his title. However, his influence on the breed was tremendous through his two sons, Ch. Dorcas Glorious of Slat and Dorcas Timberscombe Topper (2 CCs, the result of a father to daughter mating). Joan Gill incorporated Dorcas into the Westley breeding lines. Dorcas Timberscombe Topper was the sire of Joan Tudor's first great foundation sire, Ch. Camrose Fantango. Ch. Dorcas Glorious of Slat was the sire of F.T. Ch. Stubblesdown Larry, foundation sire of a Field Trial dynasty. Dorcas Leola was the foundation of the important northern kennel, Beauchasse, breeder of Boltby Kymba, who was the foundation sire of the influential northern Boltbys. Mrs Minter's lovely Stenbury bitch line went on to greater heights when in-bred into Boltby, for Kymba was out of Dorcas Leola by Sh. Ch. Torrdale Kim of Stenbury – and both Stenbury and Boltby had a background of Torrdale. Dorcas Aurora was the foundation bitch of the Deerflite's Dorcas Clorinda, foundation of the Rosecotts.

OUTCROSSING

This involves mating your bitch to a dog who is not related to her at all, with no dogs in common on a five-generation pedigree, but both dogs registered Golden Retrievers. Of course, you will find some dogs the same if you research the pedigrees further back, but they would have no influence on the mating. You may get one good animal in this way, in the first generation, but then you would have to line-breed to fix type, and, if both sire and dam are of mediocre lines, where do you go from there? I remember, years ago, seeing in a Northern Golden Retriever Year Book a famous breeder's advert, stating: "Bred right to breed right."

SOME POINTS TO WATCH FOR

1. Start planning what method of breeding you are going to do when you first get your bitch, remembering it is best to mate a bitch in her third season, or when she is about two years old. Do not rush into a decision. Pedigree-wise and construction-wise, the dog must complement the bitch, so pedigree, conformation, and temperament of the dog you choose must all go together.

2. Do not use a Champion just because he is a top dog and everybody else has used him.

3. Look at your own stock and see the faults, think for yourself and have a clear picture of what you are doing now, why you are doing it, and what you will do in the future.

4. Decide what you want to keep from the litter as part of your breeding plan, otherwise you will end up with more Goldens than you can cope with very quickly. From the beginning set a limit on your numbers. You do not need a big kennel to be a top breeder, exhibitor, or worker.

5. Look at the pedigrees of the top breeders in the strain you have bought from, and work out the methods they have used. A strain is a long-standing family within a breed, its success depends on all members being sound in construction, with typical heads, outlines and general appearance. Temperament must be good, and there should be a history of clear eye certificates, and good hip scores, and dogs should reproduce themselves in like moulds in different ownerships.

6. It is not only the sire that is of prime importance – you should aim for a strong line of bitches combined with good sires.

PLANNING THE MATING

Once you have chosen the dog you wish to use, contact the stud dog owner, as most dogs are at stud to approved bitches only, and so the owner will want to know something about your bitch. You must give details of her breeding, her hip score, and the date of her latest eye certificate (this must be up-to-date). The stud dog owner may want to see your bitch, or may have seen her at shows. You need to know the stud fee, and the stud dog owner will ask you when you think your bitch is due in season, and to make contact on the first day of her season. This is important, for a popular stud dog is often booked up. You pay for the act of mating, but it is usual for the stud dog owner to offer a free mating if the bitch misses. However, that is up to the owner of the stud dog and should not be taken for granted.

OWNING A STUD DOG

Most people wish to show and then breed, and therefore start out with a bitch. You may breed a litter in which there is a promising dog puppy and you decide, against all advice, to keep the dog and use him at stud. You will be able to use this dog on your own bitches, thus saving money, time and travelling expenses. However, this is a short-sighted policy, because it is not really viable to keep a stud dog for so few bitches, as your dogs become too closely related.

Your stud dog is only likely to get bookings from other bitches if he is of great quality, capable of winning top awards and becoming a Champion, and is from proven bloodlines. If your dog does not match up to this, he may get a few bookings from local bitches, but is not a good idea to start a dog on a stud career unless he is going to be used regularly.

Stud dog management is a skill in itself. Golden Retriever stud dogs, unlike some breeds, live well together. After a dog has served a bitch, all he needs is a wipe down with mild disinfectant, before he rejoins the other dogs. However, you will need separate facilities when bitches are in season. People do manage with males and females in the house, but this does make life difficult. Dogs have been known to chew their way through doors to get to the bitch in season. The separate facilities include exercising areas, so that the males cannot smell the odour of in-season bitches. The odour does not only come from the vaginal discharge but also from the bitch's urine, and if a male is constantly sexually excited, he will soon lose condition. Make sure your dog has up-to-date eye certificates and his hips are scored.

Ideally, you first use your dog at stud when he is just over a year old. The bitch should be a wise, kind matron who has been mated before and knows what it is all about and does not object. As the stud dog becomes more proficient, he can take on the more difficult bitches.

WHAT MAKES AN OUTSTANDING SIRE?

Obviously time helps in the judgements, but one point is clear: whatever the quality of the bitch, the top-quality sire will tend to throw something better. Of course, the problem is then where do you take the outstanding sire's daughters to to carry on your breeding line?

Ch. Michael of Moreton: A great sire of the 1930s.

Thomas Fall.

Since 1911 when the Kennel Club officially gave the breed classification as a separate variety of Retrievers under the title Golden or Yellow Retrievers, history shows us a line of outstanding sires judged by their records. Elma Stonex traced back through extended pedigrees that almost all the breed today goes back to four matings which took place between 1920 and 1925, and the greatest sires trace back directly, or later on many times, to these matings. The four crucial matings were:

1. Glory of Fyning to Stagden Cross Pamela
2. Dual Ch. Balcombe Boy to Balcombe Bunty
3. Binks of Kentford to Balvaig
4. Rory of Bentley to Aurora

Ch. Davie Of Yelme: His importance became apparent in his offspring's progeny. Thomas Fall.

Early great sires were: Ch. Cornelius (b.13.6.21), sire of three Champions, two Sh.Champions and one Field Trial Champion. His brother, Ch. Flight of Kentford, whose stud career was cut short because he was exported to India where he became an Indian Dual Champion, sired two British Champions, and one Sh.Champion. Ch. Cubbington Diver (b.23.10.24) sired five Champions. Ch. Diver of Woolley (b.29.3.27) sired four Champions and one Sh.Champion. Ch. Michael of Moreton (b.10.2.25) sired seven Champions, and one Show Champion, Gilder (b.31.7.29) not a title holder himself, but the sire of eight Champions.

Since the 1940s, sires who must be graded influential are Ch. Dorcas Glorious of Slat, who sired a 'double' Dual Champion England and Ireland, one Field Trial Champion and two Champions. Dorcas Timberscombe Topper sired five Champions. Ch. Torrdale Happy Lad sired two Champions, one Sh.Champion. Ch. Colin of Rosecott sired six Champions. Ch. Boltby Skylon sired four Sh.Champions and one Champion. Ch. Boltby Moonraker sired three Champions and two Sh.Champions. Ch. Camrose Fantango sired five Champions and one Sh.Champion. Ch. Camrose Tallyrand of Anbria sired seven Champions and one Sh.Champion. Ch. William of Westley sired three Champions and one Sh.Champion. Ch. Camrose Nicolas of Westley sired six Champions. Ch. Cabus Cadet sired five Champions and one Sh.Champion. Ch. Cabus Boltby Combine sired six Sh.Champions and one Champion. Ch. Stolford Happy Lad sired five Champions and two Sh.Champions.

Ch. Nortonwood Faunus: A son of the great Ch. Camrose Cabus Christopher, and an outstanding sire in his own right.

Ch. Sansue Golden Ruler: A top sire of the 1980s and 1990s.   *David Bull.*

The greatest sire of them all, who was also at one stage the breed record holder, was Ch. Camrose Cabus Christopher (b.17.9.67). He was a combination of southern and northern bloodlines (Ch. Camrose Tallyrand of Anbria – Cabus Boltby Charmer). He sired twenty-six title holders in the UK and many overseas title holders. Many years after his death, with artificial insemination, his son Mjaerumhogda's Thor to Camrose was born 9.10.88 and won his first CC in 1992 – so it could become twenty-seven Champions or Sh.Champions.

Another influential stud of the eighties has been the Christopher son, Ch. Nortonwood Faunus, sire of nineteen title holders in the UK and also many title holders abroad. Another Christopher son, Ch. Camrose Fabius Tarquin, has sired twelve Champions or Sh.Champions in the UK plus many abroad. The present CC record holder, with 42 CCs, is Ch. Styal Scott of Glengilde who has sired seven title holders in the UK.

Two great stud dogs of the late eighties and early nineties, whose records are not yet complete, are Ch. Gaineda Consolidator of Sansue, sire of eleven title holders in the UK, and his son, Ch. Sansue Golden Ruler, sire of nine British title holders, and both are sires of many overseas winners. A Faunus son, Sh.Ch. Stirchley Saxon, sire to date of six Sh.Champions in the UK looks to be doing well, as does Ch. Moorquest Mugwump with four title holders in the UK.

Some sires, who have not, at first, had an obvious impact, have often shown their importance when their daughters have been mated by what they have thrown. They include: Ch. Noranby Campfire, Normanby Balfour, Ch. Davie of Yelme, Ch. Donkelve Rusty, Ch. Hazelgilt, Torrdale Tinker, Sh.Ch. Torrdale Kim of Stenbury, Boltby Kymba, Stubbings Golden Dandylyon, Dorcas Bruin, Ch. Alresford Advertiser, Ch. Simon of Westley, Ch. Camrose Lucius, Ch. Davern Figaro, Ch. Sansue Camrose Phoenix, Ch. Westley Topic of Sansue, Sh.Ch. Nortonwood Checkmate, Sh.Ch. Westley Munro of Nortonwood.

The great Field Trial sires have, in the years since the 1950s, been dominated by Mrs Atkinson's Holway's. Previously, pre-war was more the time of the dual-purpose sire and the Anningsley sires were prominent. From the 1950s F.T. Ch.Muzurka of Wynford, F.T.Ch.Stubblesdown Larry, F.T.Ch.Holway Zest, F.T.Ch.Holway Westhyde Zeus, and F.T.Ch.Holway Denier have built up fine records. At the present time F.T.Ch. Holway Corbiere is proving an influential sire.

TOP BROOD BITCHES

Obviously, it is not as easy for a brood bitch to show her influence by the tremendous number of her titled children; a dog has so much more of a chance with the number of bitches he can mate. However, in the early 1900s two bitches literally laid the foundation for the breed today. Yellow Nell was bred by D. MacDonald-Ingestre (the Earl of Shrewsbury's head keeper) and owned by H. Hall. She was born in 1908, sired by Ingestre Scamp out of Ingestre Tyne. the other bitch was Normanby Beauty, acquired by Mrs Charlsworth in 1906, of unknown pedigree. Sh.Ch. Noranby Dandelion (Ingestre Dred – Ingestre Luna, b.1913) was also behind so many influential sires and dams. Noranby Judith, Ch. Vic of Woolley and Heydown Bertha were the dams of three Champions each. Sh. Ch. Sewardstone Tess was the dam of four Champions and one Sh.Champion.

After the Second World War Stubbings Golden Olympia founded a dual-purpose dynasty – one daughter, Dual Ch. Stubbledown Golden Lass produced two Field Trial Champions and two CC winners and founded a Field Trial Dynasty. Olympia's other daughter was Ch. Braconlea Gaiety. The Stenbury bitch line is famous, largely due to Mrs Minter's skill and to her bitch, Laughter of Stenbury, born in the 1940s, dam of two Stenbury Champions and behind other Stenbury title holders up to the present.

Ch. Westley Victoria: Top brood bitch of all time in the UK.   *Sally Anne Thompson.*

Ch. Dukeries Dancing Lady: Foundation dam of the Torrdales in the 1930s.

Thomas Fall.

Three Dorcas bitches founded strains: Dorcas Leola dam of Ch. Beauchasse Gaiety, Sh.Ch. Beauchasse Bergarnot, and Boltby's Kymba (2 CCs) sire of the great Boltby sires, Ch's Skylon and Moonraker. Dorcas Clorinda was behind the Rosecotts, and Dorcas Aurora foundation of the Deerflites. Westley Frolic of Yelme was dam of three Champions, and Ch. Susan of Westley was dam of two influential dogs – Int.Dual Ch. David of Westley and Ch. William of Westley.

A line of influential Camrose dams started with the foundation bitch Golden Camrose Tess, who was grandam of Ch. Camrose Tantara, dam of three Champions. Camrose Wistansy was the dam of two Champions and one Sh.Champion, and Cabus Boltby Charmer was the dam of three Champions. Ch. Styal Susila was an important dam, producing one Champion and three Sh.Champions. Styal Sonnet of Gyrima only had one litter, but in it were two Champions and one Sh.Champion.

The greatest brood bitch in the breed to date is Ch. Westley Victoria, dam of four Champions and four Sh.Champions. Sh.Ch. Linchael Delmoss had two Sh.Champions and one Champion. Ch. Nomis Portia of Stenbury had three Sh.Champions and one Champion. Sh.Ch. Sansue Wrainbow had three Champions and one Sh.Champion. Rossbourne Party Piece of Sansue had three Sh.Champions.

Other bitches who have shown their influence within their strains include: Trixie of Milldam, foundation of the Elsivilles. Ch. Briar of Arbrook, foundation of the Anbrias. Sh.Ch. Whamstead Emerald, foundation of the Milos. Annette of Carrow is behind the Janvilles. Stolford Brecklands Senorita is behind many Stolfords. Ch. Alresford Mall is dam of Ch. Alresford Advertiser. Gainspa Sabina is behind the Gainspa's Sh.Champions. Sh. Ch. Boltby Sugar Bush is dam of Ch. Cabus Boltby Combine. Sh. Ch. Peatling Stella of Teecon is behind the Teecons. Sh. Ch. Pandown Poppet of Yeo is dam of Ringmaster of Yeo. Ch. Deerflite Endeavour of Yeo is behind many Yeo

A top brood bitch Ch. Linchael Delmoss (left), and her daughter Linchael Chantilly.

bitches, foundations for many kennels. The three litter sisters, Ch. Gyrima Pippalina, Ch. Gyrima Pipparanda – foundation of Ninell, Sandusky and Darris, and the third sister, Sh.Ch. Gyrima Pipparetta continued the Gyrima title holders. The other important bitch for Gyrima was Sh. Ch. Romside Raffeena of Gyrima. Irish Ch. Mandingo Marigold is behind the Glenavis. Sh.Ch. Rachenco Charnez of Gaineda is behind the Gaineda line. The Davern foundation bitches are Camrose Flavella (dam of Astella of Davern) and Ch. Camrose Pruella of Davern. Sh. Ch. Sinnhein Minutemaid is behind the present-day Sinnheins. Ch. Beauchasse Gaiety is behind the Fordvales and Rossbournes. Lindy Lantern is behind the Lindys.

FIELD TRIAL DAMS
Again, since the 1980s, the Holway bitches have played a very important part in the Field Trial strains. Mention must be made of Dual Ch. Stubblesdown Golden Lass, dam of F.T.Ch. Stubblesdown Larry and F.T.Ch. Westhyde Stubblesdown Major, both founder sires of Field Trial dynasties. This leads us to F.T.Ch. Musicmaker of Yeo (b.29.5.47) bred by Lucille Sawtell, and making her a member of that rare club that has bred Champions and F.T.Champions. She was the

foundation bitch of the Holways, for when mated to F.T.Ch.Westhyde Stubblesdown Major she produced the great F.T. Ch. Mazurka of Wynford. Westhyde Merry Lass was dam of three F.T. Champions. F.T.Ch. Holway Flush of Yeo produced many Champion Field Trial dogs. F.T.Ch. Little Marston Chorus of Holway was dam of F.T.Ch. Holway Corbiere and F.T.Ch. Holway Crosa. Strathcarron Seil of Standerwick was foundation dam of the successful Standerwick working lines, dam of two F.T.Champions and one Champion. Her daughter, F.T.Ch.Standerwick Roberta of Abnells has herself produced F.T.Ch. Abnells Hilary of Standerwick.

Westley and Standerwick have done what has never been done since after the Second World War – two of their bitches have produced a F.T.Champion and a Champion, namely Echo of Westley, dam of F.T. Champion Holway Teal of Westley, and also Champion Pippa of Westley (17 CCs). Strathcarron Seil of Standerwick is dam of F.T.Ch. Standerwick Rumbustuous of Catcombe and F.T.Ch. Standerwick Roberta of Abnalls and also Ch. Standerwick Thomasina.

AMERICAN BLOODLINES
The Golden Retriever Club of America have a Hall of Fame for outstanding sires and dams. Dating back to the 1930s, Am. Can. Ch. Speedwell Pluto was highly influential in the early development of the breed. Bingo of Yelme held both English and American titles, and he is behind many American pedigrees as the sire of Gilnockie Coquette, who was born in 1938. This bitch left an indelible mark on the bloodlines of American Golden Retrievers. Am. Can. Ch. Golden Knolls King Alphonzo was a well-known sire of the 1950s, siring a total of thirty-three Champions – sixteen were out of Ch. Chee Chee of Sprucewood. His line-bred granddaughter, Ch. Sprucewood's Harvest Sugar produced sixteen title-holders, who were the foundation for several modern kennels.

Ch. Sunsets Happy Duke, born 1964, owned and bred by Charles Cronheim, was a handsome big-winning dog and he produced two highly influential sons – Ch. Misty Morns Sunset CD TD WC and Am. Can. Ch. Cummings Gold Rush Charlie. Sunset produced more than 130 Show Champions and Obedience and Utility dogs. His half-brother, the great winner Ch. Cummings

Am. Can. Ch. Amberac's Asterling Aruba: Top-producing bitch in the USA, with thirty Champion offspring to her credit. J. Luria.

Gold Rush Charlie was not only a beautiful specimen, but also sired Champions in double figures. Many of the Cragmount Golden Retrievers were influential sires, and many of today's top winners include Cragmount dogs in their pedigrees. Am. Can. Mex. Ber. Ch. Beckwith's Copper Coin sired fifteen Champions, and their Am. Can. Ch. Beckwith's Frolic of Yeo CDX was the dam of twelve Champions. Other kennel names that appear at the back of pedigrees of present-day winners are: Lorelei, Des Lacs, Sprucewood, Golden Knoll and Featherquest.

A top sire, Ch. Goldcoast Here Comes The Sun CD, produced among his successful offspring a daughter, Am. Can. Ch. Amberac's Asterling Aruba, who became the dam of thirty Champions. Ch. Kyrie Daemon Am, CDX, WC has made his mark, and the stud dogs of the Goldrush kennels have had a big effect on the breed.

Looking at the pedigrees of working-bred Golden Retrievers, there are a number of kennel prefixes that appear time and again. One in particular is the Tigathoe prefix owned by Mrs George Flinn of Connecticut. This kennel was started in the forties and has enjoyed unparalleled success. Of the thirteen Field Champions bred or owned by this kennel, two were Dual Champions. Included among the kennel's winners and producers are Ch. Joe of Tigathoe FC, AFC, Canadian FC Bonnie Brooks Elmer, and the great dam, Tigathoe's Chicksaw.

The Topbrass kennel started in 1967 and the Mertens built up a family line for all disciplines, although concentrating more on Field and Obedience dogs. FC AFC Topbrass Cotton was the National Amateur Champion in 1985. Barbara Howard's AFC Holway Barty has been influential on Field and Obedience lines, and the Belvedere kennel owned by Mercedes Hitchcock has contributed to working lines.

BUYING STOCK

Buyers are rather looked down upon by breeders, more so by the not very successful breeders. A buyer who, for various reasons, wishes to stay so and not become a breeder has to have an excellent eye for a dog. In the end a buyer has to be a better judge than the breeder, often seeing in the rough that there is the potential for greatness. Buyers are not linked to one strain only, but will see the good points in all strains. So the best of luck, be you breeder or buyer – here's to your first Champion!

Chapter Eleven

MATING, WHELPING AND REARING

THE BROOD BITCH

The bitch has four phases in the oestrous cycle:

1. ANOESTRUS: A time of sexual inactivity; the span of an average cycle is about seventy-five days, but this is variable.

2. PRO-OESTRUS: The start of vaginal bleeding. The bitch is not usually sexually receptive. Length of cycle varies, averaging nine to thirteen days. This is when we say the bitch has started her season.

3. OESTRUS: This is the time of acceptance. The vaginal discharge sometimes becomes less bloody, and can become colourless. Length of cycle varies, averaging nine days.

4. METOESTRUS: This stage occurs in the unmated bitch, the average length of cycle is ninety days.

It is important to remember that with animals so much is variable, and your bitch never seems to fit in with the textbook scenario. However, if we understand the most normal course of events, bearing in mind possible variations, a reasonably clear pattern should emerge.

PLANNING A LITTER

The average age for the start of puberty in dogs is six to seven months. but it is often as late as twenty-two months. Golden Retrievers do not usually have their first season until they are nine months of age. After the first season, a bitch usually comes into season about every nine months.

You should never mate a bitch until she is at least twenty-two months old, and it is advisable to wait until she is two years old. I would advise you not to delay later than five years for a first litter, and in the UK you cannot mate a bitch of eight years old without special permission from the Kennel Club. Bitches should never be mated on following seasons after they have had a reasonable-sized litter, and I believe that if a bitch has three litters in her lifetime, that is enough.

THE IN-SEASON BITCH

Just before the start of a season, many bitches start passing small amounts of urine, at frequent intervals, when they are outside. If you are planning to mate your bitch is important not to miss the beginning of the season, so check for blood-stained discharge by pressing a white tissue against the bitch's vulva every morning and evening. Some bitches are so clean they lick any pre-signs away. The first obvious signs are a swollen vulva and a blood-stained discharge. From now on, you must keep your bitch away from males, although, at this stage, she would not allow them to mate her. On the first day of the season, telephone the owner of the stud dog you have previously made contact with and decided to use.

WHEN TO MATE?

The twelfth day to the fourteenth day seems to be a good average for a successful mating. The physical signs are a very enlarged vulva, which is often soft – but not always. The discharge is straw-coloured rather than blood-stained. The bitch's behaviour will also change. If you have other bitches and they sniff her, she will stand and turn her tail to one side, showing a readiness to be mated. If you do not have any other bitches, stroke down your bitch's spine and the base of the tail; she will, again, move her tail to one side.

The correct date for mating can be ascertained by the vet taking a vaginal smear from your bitch. By looking at the types of cell present and their relative preponderance, your vet can tell the stage of the cycle. However, a series of smears taken at forty-eight hourly intervals, from about nine to ten days, is needed to pinpoint the right day. Another method which is gaining in popularity, is a blood test, taken from about seven to ten days, to measure progesterone levels in the blood. After examination, your vet will recommend the best day for mating. I think it can be generally agreed that the majority of bitches are mated too early because their owners panic and think they will take them too late.

THE MATING

So the day is decided, and you have made a firm booking with the owner of the stud dog. Make sure your bitch has a chance to urinate before you reach the stud dog, and make sure she is wearing a collar, as you will probably need to hold her steady during the mating. It is important to remember that this is a completely new experience, and even the most placid bitch may find it frightening. The stages of mating are:

1. Make sure the bitch is wearing a collar and is on the lead.
2. Check the bitch is ready for mating.
3. Let the dog meet the bitch, and allow sniffing and a little controlled flirting.
4. Once the dog mounts the bitch, you can breathe a sigh of relief, and ask the bitch's handler to hold her steady by her collar. Even the nicest of bitches will move at the wrong moment, so the handler must face the bitch, holding her collar at each side.

The 'ideal' bitch stands still, tail held to one side and hindquarters braced. The stud dog owner will help the dog, with one arm under the bitch supporting her, so she does not sag or pull away at the vital moment. The dog when he has mounted the bitch penetrates the vulva with his penis while holding her round her waist. The stud dog owner may gently hold her vulva to ensure the dog is entering in the correct direction. A little Vaseline can be put on to the vulva which helps in the penetration.

The second ejaculation of the dog, which is one minute after penetration, contains the sperm and the dog at this stage is making strong thrusting movements with his penis. The third part of the process consists of a lot of fluid which is ejaculated intermittently during the tie and helps transport the sperm. Then follows the tie, during which the swollen bulbus penis of the dog remains inside the bitch's vagina and the dog and bitch are held together – the time of the tie varies from five minutes to one hour. I have found that increasingly, older dogs tie for a shorter period.

The owner of the dog usually turns the male carefully so he is not resting on the bitch and they are standing back to back. This is when a stool for you to sit on comes in useful, because you must hold the pair together until the tie breaks spontaneously. If you do not do this, the bitch can become bored and try to pull away and drag the dog around. When they break away sometimes there is quite a lot of prostatic fluid in evidence; this does not contain sperm and is nothing to worry about. You can have puppies even if a tie does not take place, provided the dog's penis has remained within the bitch for a few minutes after ejaculation.

THE STUD FEE

You will be expected to pay the stud fee after the first mating. The stud dog owner might ask you to bring your bitch's eye and hip documentation, and, likewise, you can ask to see the stud dog's papers. You will be given a copy of the the dog's pedigree and the form, signed by the stud dog owner, for litter registration. Sometimes a second mating is offered, but this must be no later than forty-eight hours from the first mating. Find out from the stud dog owner if your bitch will be offered a repeat mating if she fails to come into whelp. Remember, you pay for the services of the dog and not for the actual litter, so you do not get a refund.

If you are using a young, unproven stud dog, the terms may be that you pay an agreed amount when the bitch has puppies. Some stud dog owners will ask for their choice of the puppies instead of the stud fee, i.e. 'the pick of the litter'. This can lead to complications, and I would advise you to pay the stud fee.

Do not think you can now relax your attention as regards your in-season bitch. She could be mated again by another dog, if you are careless. So the same level of care is necessary until the season is finished.

PREGNANCY

At one time, it was always said the length of pregnancy was sixty-three days from the day of mating. Research has now shown sixty days to be more accurate, but it can range from fifty-seven to seventy-two days. You do not need to change your bitch's diet for four weeks after the mating. The foetuses are small, and a large litter will make little demands on the bitch. At twenty to twenty-one days after mating, the embryo begins to change shape and attaches itself to the walls of the uterine horns.

The following fourteen days are vital to the prospective litter, which at this stage are very susceptible to anything that happens to the bitch, i.e. infection, certain medications, live vaccination, accidents etc. So it is important at this time (three to five weeks in whelp) not to go to shows, to training classes or take your bitch on long car journeys.

How do you tell if your bitch is in whelp? Between twenty to thirty days after mating, a vet can feel the tiny marble-sized foetuses in the uterus, like a row of beads. If your bitch has not had a litter before, her teats can become enlarged and bright-pink. The personality of the bitch can change; she starts to look after herself, and she may start to cling to you. The bitch can be scanned by an electronic scanner to see if she in whelp and how many puppies she is carrying, though this may not be so accurate. The most noticeable physical sign is abdominal enlargement, which starts with a slight filling out in the flanks and progresses steadily.

Towards the end of the pregnancy when the uterine horns are becoming full, they cannot continue to lie parallel, so they fold back and drop lower into the abdomen, making the bitch's outline change. The mammary glands begin to enlarge, and from about the thirty-fifth day there will be a discharge of clear or white mucus from the vagina. If there is any dark discharge, consult your vet at once. Some bitches have a type of morning sickness and cannot eat till about lunch time.

FEEDING THE PREGNANT BITCH

The first change you need to make to the diet is during the fifth week when you need to add a small amount of extra food, and divide the food into two meals a day. During the sixth week increase food twenty-five per cent over the usual maintenance level, by the seventh week it should be thirty per cent over the usual maintenance level, and by the eighth week, forty per cent over the usual maintenance level. Your bitch will draw from her own body stores if the extra food is not given. The important point is feed to keep your bitch in good condition, at her ideal body weight. Excess food intake only adds weight to the bitch, and excess weight at whelping can create complications.

The extra food should be protein. The pregnant bitch should not have food of high bulk with little nutritive value. By the time she is seven weeks in whelp, it is often a good idea to give the food in three meals. Additives (vitamins, minerals, etc.) constitute part of many modern feeds, especially the complete feeds that are designed for the in-whelp bitch. Do not be tempted to add more and more supplements, as too much or too many additives can do a lot of harm. Over-supplementation with calcium and vitamin D can lead to problems, and it does not help to guard against eclampsia – a post-whelping problem of lowered levels of calcium in the blood. If a bitch suffers from this condition, a vet is needed to give intravenous and subcutaneous injections of calcium and glucose. The condition is fatal unless treated.

EXERCISE

Normal exercise can continue throughout the greater part of the pregnancy, with limited exercise up to the day of whelping. Let the bitch go at her own pace and do not allow jumping or rough play. Good muscular development and tone are essential in pregnancy to keep the bowels regular, the circulation going, and to aid whelping.

WORMING

Modern wormers are safe, and it is advisable to worm your bitch during pregnancy. Ask your vet to prescribe a worming programme that is suitable for the in-whelp bitch.

PREPARATIONS FOR WHELPING

You will need to decide well in advance where your bitch will whelp. She must have comfortable accommodation, and she must be used to it. Do not make the mistake of bringing a kennel-bitch in the night before she is due to whelp, or putting a house dog out in a kennel just before she whelps. A utility room is ideal, and this must be prepared in good time so that your bitch has a chance to get used to a whelping box. A bitch often has her own ideas about where to whelp. Her favoured places are usually highly unsuitable, and usually entail a great amount of digging – a primitive part of the cycle.

The room should be heated. Heat lamps are not so popular nowadays. I have always found that if the lamp is warm enough for the puppies, it is too warm for the dam. You can have the lamp suspended over a corner of the box for the puppies only. If you are using a lamp, remember it must be high enough so that the bitch can stand up without touching it.

If you plan to breed a few litters, you can buy or make your own whelping box. It must be large enough for your bitch to stretch out comfortably (4 ft by 4 ft) with the sides and back over 2 ft. high. The front should be in removable sections so that, at first, when the puppies are very young, the bitch can step in and out easily, but as the puppies get older, you can put another section in to stop them getting out. It is a good idea to have a rail around the inside of the box, across the back and on two sides. This stops the bitch from lying on the puppies by mistake and crushing them. It can be removed after the first four days.

I have also seen large cardboard boxes being used, like those that refrigerators and televisions come in. The box is cut to shape, and a further box is placed as a hood, which gives the covered den the bitch is, ideally, searching for. If you are planning only one litter, the advantage of the cardboard box is that it can be thrown away when you have finished with it. As the puppies get older, the bitch must have space to get away from them. During the second week, or earlier, she will start to lie out of the box, going back in to feed her puppies. Bitches vary so much that no hard and fast rules can be made, but one point must always be remembered – as the puppies grow, the bitch must have space to get away from them, if necessary.

During the last fortnight of your bitch's pregnancy, if she is heavy she might find it necessary to urinate more, as the full uterus is pressing on the urinary bladder. Do not scold her if she asks to go out in the middle of the night, or if she has an overnight lapse. These last two weeks are the time to get all the equipment you will need for the whelping: hot-water bottles, suitable disinfectant, towelling, polyester fabric and newspapers, sharp scissors, milk powder suitable for new-born pups and puppy feeder – hopefully, you will not need the last two, but imagine trying to buy them on a Sunday! In the last week, wash round the bitch's teats with warm water, with a little antiseptic solution added.

WHELPING

THE FIRST STAGE

Whelping is a natural and normal process, and Golden Retrievers are usually easy whelpers and make marvellous mothers. Normal pregnancies last from sixty to sixty-three days, but puppies born from the fifty-sixth day usually live. Whelping is usually in three stages. The first stage varies in time. It can go on for as long as forty-eight hours, but the average is between six and twenty hours. This is the phase in which the bitch prepares for the birth, and you know it by its behavioural signs. As long as the bitch knows where you are, it is better to get on with doing a job in the house, such as cleaning out cupboards. The signs are restlessness, bed-making, panting, refusing food, and digging – and as long as you keep a very firm eye on the digging, this is all part of the natural process. At this stage, the bitch can have a far-away look.

All the signs should become progressively more vigorous and continuous. If they do not, it could be the first sign of uterine inertia. It is not a bad idea to ring your veterinary practice: you will already have told them the due date, and it is useful if the vet is on standby as the first stage gets underway. There is no certain way of knowing when whelping will commence. However, the most reliable guide is a drop in the bitch's temperature. The temperature of a bitch in the last weeks of pregnancy is below average 100 degrees Fahrenheit (37.7 degrees Centigrade), but at the onset of whelping, the temperature drops to 97-99 degrees Fahrenheit (37 degrees Centigrade). However, the temperature may stay at this level for only a few hours, so you need to take the temperature twice a day. First-stage labour should start within twenty-four hours of the low temperature being recorded, and I have always found this to be the case with my bitches.

THE SECOND STAGE

Throughout pregnancy, your bitch will probably have had a little mucoid discharge from the vulva, and this now increases in volume. In the first stage of labour, the cervix (birth passage) has softened or dilated to allow the puppies to pass from the uterus down the vagina, and out. So, in

Sh.Ch. Westley Clementina with her four-day-old puppies.

the second stage the cervix is fully dilated, and now your bitch is pushing down in abdominal contractions. You must watch carefully: the contractions can be a ripple, then a push. Take note what time the contractions start, and if the bitch has been straining for two hours and no puppy has appeared, contact your vet.

The next tangible sign can be the appearance at the vulva of a black, fluid bag. This membrane has surrounded each puppy during gestation and has now helped to lubricate it out. This water bag may have burst inside the bitch, and then the contents gush out. The bag does not contain a puppy, but there should be one not far behind. Your bitch may stand, sit, or lie down in the whelping box for the birth. The puppy should slide out quickly; it is inside a thin bag of membrane that has its own placenta or afterbirth attached to the umbilical cord. The puppy is usually born head-first, but often it is hind-feet first. A breech birth is a puppy presenting rump-first, with hind legs tucked under the body.

The bitch will usually break the bag, freeing the puppy, and she will cut through the umbilical cord with her teeth. She will eat the placenta, and she will then set about resuscitating the puppy – and she will do this quite roughly. Ideally, the bitch will all this herself, but if she does not seem to know what to do, you must intervene. You will need to remove the membrane around the puppy's mouth first, for until that is done it cannot breathe. The umbilical cord should be cut about two to three inches from the puppy. Rub the puppy with a towel to dry it, and then present it to the bitch who will lick it, and then put it on a teat to feed. Veterinary investigation subscribes to the belief that when the bitch eats the placentas it stimulates the milk to flow and helps the uterus to go back to its normal size. In the wild, the afterbirths would be the bitch's food for several days.

The interval between births varies, but in most cases the bitch has two or three puppies at short intervals of ten to thirty minutes, followed by a rest of one to two hours before repeating the process. If the bitch is straining and no puppies have arrived after two hours, consult your vet. Some breeders recommend that puppies are kept in a separate box until whelping is over. The box should be kept warm with a towelling-covered hot-water bottle. However, I think this can upset

For the first ten days the mother will feed and clean up after her puppies.

the bitch. Generally, she will be quite happy to clean and nurse the puppies between births and will keep the whelping area clean. Whelping on the veterinary-type polyester fur, with newspapers underneath, helps to keep the area dry. You can put the puppies on the towel-covered hot-water bottle in a corner of the box while a new pup is being born and attended to.

If a Caesarean becomes necessary following the birth of some puppies, or because of uterine inertia, leave the puppies in a warm box while the bitch is taken to the surgery. They will come to no harm without food for a few hours. The use of modern anaesthetics means that the bitch is awake as soon as the operation is over. When she returns, make her comfortable in the whelping box, and as soon as she recognises the sound of her crying puppies, they can be put back with her. Once she has licked them all, full mothering behaviour will follow. It is a good idea to smear the puppies with a little of the bitch's vaginal discharge to make them truly hers, and stay with her until the pups are suckling and she is mothering them.

THE THIRD STAGE

The third stage is the stage in which the afterbirths are expelled, after the birth of the puppy. Bitches, therefore, alternate between stages two and three. During the whelping offer your bitch drinks of milk and glucose and, if it has been a long whelping and she appears tired, add a teaspoon of brandy to the milk. Do not offer food.

AFTER CARE OF BITCH AND PUPPIES

How do you know it is all over? Many bitches become relaxed and go to sleep. Your vet should call to see the bitch on the day following the whelping to check the uterus is empty and that the bitch has no sign of infection. An injection of Oxytocin is often given so that the uterus contracts down properly, ensuring nothing has been left in it. You will find your bitch has a greenish discharge for about twenty-four hours followed by a brownish-red discharge, which gradually lessens over several weeks. However, if you get a blackish, foul-smelling discharge, contact your vet at once. You must see that the puppies are warm enough, for the first thirty-six hours after the birth are the most critical of their lives. A newborn puppy's body temperature is low compared with an adult. The bitch must have peace and quiet, so no visitors should be allowed at this stage. You must take your bitch outside to relieve herself, as she will be reluctant to leave her puppies. You also need to keep a close check to ensure the bitch does not lie on any of the puppies; so for the first three nights it is a good idea to sleep on a camp bed in the bitch's quarters.

The bitch's diet must be light for the first twenty-four hours. Offer scrambled egg, fish, milk and plenty of clean water, and feed her in the box at first. Remember, good food helps to make good puppies. After twenty-four hours she can go back to her normal diet, but make sure this includes protein-rich foods not carbohydrates, and increase the amount until she is having about three times her maintenance diet. It is better to feed this as three separate meals. If you feed a complete food, use the diet formulated for nursing bitches and feed as per the instructions. This will contain all the additives your bitch will need. If you are feeding canned food, check the label to see what additives are included, and if you are feeding cooked frozen chicken or tripe, calcium and vitamin supplements must be given.

With large litters of nine or more, check that all the puppies are getting milk. If necessary, you can top-up with a special milk supplement, available from your vet or from a pet store If you have a smaller litter, check the milk ducts do not become too hard or full, which can lead to mastitis. If there is a tendency to hardness, take a warm cloth, hold it gently on to the area and then express the milk from them. Bitches vary in how long they stay with their puppies. After the first four days they will start to stay out of the box for longer periods. At the end of the first week, cut the tip of the puppies' nails, and remember to do this once a week from now onwards, otherwise the pups will scratch the bitch. If the bitch is feeding nine puppies or more, you can almost feed her as much as she wants. You wean your puppies from two-and-a-half to three-and-a-half weeks, depending on the size of the litter. Before you wean, you need to worm your puppies. I use a liquid wormer, which I find easier to use with puppies. You need to weigh each puppy, and I find a material bag which fits on to a balance is ideal. I weigh the bag, put the puppy into the bag and on to the hook of the balance, and then get a helper to write the weight down. Always see the bag is safe to take the weight, and do the job quickly so that the puppies do not wriggle. Most breeders worm at three, five and seven weeks, but it can be done earlier after consulting your vet.

WEANING

I find it easier to start the puppies off by eating solids, rather than to start with lapping when the litter is still suckling. I start off by offering top-quality raw minced beef (about 1 oz. per puppy), given to each puppy individually. Make sure you have a system, as it is all too easy to feed the same puppy twice. Give one meal a day for four days, and then add another meal so you are feeding morning and night, and then they can go into their mother for a drink of milk.

At four weeks you can start them lapping with a meal of prepared puppy milk and cereal. You can use a baby cereal, as long as it is not too thin a consistency. Start the puppies lapping with the food in a small saucer or tray – some learn quickly, some seem to take forever. Wipe the puppies' faces and paws with a damp flannel when they have finished. At this stage, start reducing your bitch's food, and by the time the puppies are weaned she should be back to her normal diet. By five weeks the puppies are on five meals a day:

8.00am: meat	1.30pm: milk and cereal.	9.30pm: milk/cereal.
10.30am: milk	5.30pm: meat.	

European Ch. Standfast Angus at fourteen weeks. It is essential to get puppies off to a good start by rearing on a top-quality diet.

At four weeks, the puppies should be getting 3oz. meat daily each feed, at five weeks 4oz. meat daily each feed, and up to 1 pint milk daily; at six weeks 5oz. meat daily each feed, at seven weeks 6oz. meat daily each feed, and at eight weeks 7oz. meat daily each feed.

At six weeks they can start on puppy meal or small-bite mixer, making sure it is well soaked. Puppies are usually completely weaned by six weeks and ready to go to their new homes between seven and eight weeks. At eight weeks the puppies are on four meals a day. If you are using a complete food, follow the directions for quantity, or feed 14oz. meat, 1 pint milk, 2oz. meal or mixer. At ten to twelve weeks fresh cow or goat's milk can be given. Between four and five months feeds can be cut to three daily, with increased amounts. At six months offer two meals a day; you can make it one meal at nine months or continue with two meals – by nine months the main part of their growth has been completed.

An adult Golden Retriever dog needs about 2lb. of food a day, a little less for a bitch, roughly 1lb. of meat plus 1lb. biscuit meal or equivalents. Remember to feed high-quality balanced foods, and do not add supplements to foods that already have them as part of their balance. Try to feed to a condition that you can tell by your eye and hands.

All puppies must leave for their new homes with a diet sheet, and please be careful when it comes to selling your puppies. Talk to the potential owners, find out about their lifestyle, and do not part with a puppy unless you get the right answers. Make sure the new owners realise that you will help if they have problems, and finally, assure them that, if through circumstances beyond their control, they cannot keep the dog – you must be contacted so that you can help with rehoming.

Chapter Twelve

GOLDEN RETRIEVERS IN BRITAIN

THE PIONEERS

CULHAM

The 1st Viscount Harcourt was the first to exhibit Golden Retrievers, but not under that name. Lewis Harcourt was an influential Liberal politician who, like the 2nd Lord Tweedmouth, held the highest offices of state. He was Secretary of State for the Colonies (1910-1915), First Commissioner of Works (1905-1910 and 1915-1917), and M.P. for Rossendale Division Lancs 1904-1917. An aristocrat in the great Liberal tradition, he knew the 2nd Lord Tweedmouth well and often shot at Guisachan where he would have seen the yellow retrievers. His country seat was Nuneham Park, Oxfordshire. This handsome Palladian villa was bought in 1990 to be converted into a hotel and conference centre. The photograph of Culham Brass, born 1904, retrieving to a keeper is taken at Nuneham where they kept about twenty retrievers.

Culham Brass (born 1904) retrieving to a keeper at Nuneham Park, home of the 1st Viscount Harcourt.

Thomas Fall.

A letter written by John MacLennan one of the Guisachan keepers of the time (kept by Lady Pentland, niece of the 2nd Lord Tweedmouth) states that Viscount Harcourt got the foundation of his kennel from two puppies that he sold. The dam of the puppies was out of Hon Archie Marjoribanks' Golden Retriever, Lady. He is also reputed to have acquired some Golden Retrievers from the Earl of Portsmouth.

Harcourt shot over his dogs, and in 1908 he exhibited at Crufts and the Crystal Palace, showing Culham Rossa, Culham Brass (a foundation sire), Culham Copper, and Culham Flame. They were entered as Flat or Wavy-coated Retrievers. Harcourt does not appear to have continued showing his dogs, but was still breeding in 1919 when he bred the first Dual Champion, Balcombe Boy. This dog was sired by Culham Tip, who almost has a full four-generation pedigree to his name, out of Culham Amber II, who was unregistered. Boy was a present from Lord Harcourt to Mr R. Herman. Lord Harcourt died on February 24th 1922, and his influence on the breed was incalculable.

NORANBY

Mrs Winifred Maud Charlsworth has probably done more than any other single individual to develop the Golden Retriever as a show and working dog, and her involvement in the breed spans almost fifty years, dating back to 1906. She obtained her first Golden, an unregistered bitch of unknown parentage, she registered the bitch as Normanby Beauty. In her book on the Golden Retriever, Mrs Charlsworth writes: "it was purely luck, and the influence of that great sportsman, the late Parson Upcher, that enabled me to get my first golden." Through Beauty's progeny, Mrs Charlsworth laid the foundations of the breed.

Interestingly, Mrs Charlsworth started out with the prefix Normanby, but after a mix-up in 1914 when the Crufts dog CC winner lost his award, all her dogs were registered with the Noranby prefix. She bred the first Champion, Noranby Campfire, Ch. Noranby Jeptha, and in Jeptha's litter

Ch. Noranby Diana, born 1929.

Ralph Robinson.

were: Ch. Banner and Ch. Vic of Woolley. She also bred Ch. Noranby Dutiful, and Ch. Noranby Deirdre. All these dogs gained their titles before the Second World War. Her great achievement was her last dog to show and trial, who became Dual Champion Noranby Destiny, born in 1943.

INGESTRE
About the same time as Mrs Charlsworth started in the breed, the Earl of Shrewsbury, connected by marriage to the Earl of Ilchester, acquired some Golden Retrievers from Guisachan. They were registered under the name of his headkeeper, MacDonald, but with the family's prefix, Ingestre. Some early influential dogs from this kennel, which produced very dark dogs, possibly due to Flat-coat bloodlines. They included Sh.Ch. Klip, Sh.Ch. Top Twig bred by H. Hall but out of the famous matron, Yellow Nell who was bred at Ingestre, and Sh.Ch. Noranby Dandelion.

THE BREED DEVELOPS

KENTFORD: The next kennel of note was founded in 1911 when the Hon Mrs E. Grigg (Kentford) bought her foundation, Sh.Ch. Noranby Dandelion, from Mrs Charlsworth (but bred at Ingestre). Mrs Grigg also bred or owned Ch. Bess of Kentford (first bitch Ch.), Ch. Flight of Kentford, Ft.Ch. Eredine Rufus, Ch. Kib of Kentford, Ch. Mischief of Kentford, and Ch. Rip of Kentford. She showed and trialled her dogs up to the early 1920s.

ABBOTS: Mr Jenner had his first Golden in 1917, and he went on to own or breed Ch. Noble of Quinton, Ch. Michael of Moreton, Sh.Ch. Sewardstone Tess, Sh.Ch. Abbotts Ann, Ch. Haulstone Marker, Sh.Ch. Abbotts Wisdom, Ch. Goldgleam of Aldgrove, Ch. Abbots Winkle, Ch. Abbots Music, Ch. Tickencote Jennie, Ch. Davie of Yelme, Sh.Ch. Leondor, Ch. Abbots Daisy and Ch. Dukeries Dancing Lady.

Ch. Flight of Kentford, owned by the Hon . Mrs E. Grigg.

Ch. Abbots Daisy, 1934.

Thomas Fall.

Mr Jenner's great days were prior to the Second World War. After the war he won two CCs with his Yelme bitch, and I remember meeting him at one of the Golden Retriever Club Championship Shows at Sandford on Thames, and he was both knowledgeable and kind. I remember his friend Mr Gill (Gillenches) was with him – breeder of Ch. Abbots Music and Ch. Colthill Delia – and he also owned for a time the great sire Gilder.

HEYDOWN: Lt Col the Hon Douglas Carnegie owned the Heydown Retrievers. They included: Ch. Heydown Gunner, Ch. Heydown Grip, Ch. Heydown Guider, Ch. Heydown Gillyflower, Ch. Heydown Goody-Two-Shoes. A very influential kennel.

SPEEDWELL: The Evers-Swindell's influential Speedwell kennel started in 1921 when they bought a puppy called Cornelius. He became a Champion and was also a famous sire. Other Retrievers bred or owned include: Sh.Ch. Speedwell Emerald, Ch. Speedwell Beryl, Ch. Kelso of

Aldgrove, Ch. Joseph of Housesteads, Ch. Speedwell Brandy, Ch. Speedwell Molly and Sh.Ch. Speedwell Dainty.

HAULSTONE: Mr Eccles bought his first in 1912 by accident. He answered an advert thinking he was getting a liver flatcoat. In fact she was golden, and the advertiser said she was of Tweedmouth's strain. After the Second World War Mr and Mrs Eccles were known for their workers, but pre-war they were known for their winners and workers. Their Ch. Haulstone Dan, bred by Mr R. Herman, was a lovely dog whose early photograph still does him justice. They bred Ch. Haulstone Dusty and Ch. Haulstone Marker, and owned Ch. Haulstone Sprig.

WOOLLEY: This kennel was owned Mrs Jacqueline Cottingham, a fascinating lady, who disappeared from the dog scene in the 1940s, possibly to make a new home in America. She bred or owned Ch. Reine of Woolley, Ch. Cubbington Diver, Ch. Banner of Woolley, Ch. Vic of Woolley, Ch. & Am Ch. Vesta of Woolley, Ch. Diver of Woolley, Ch. Marine of Woolley, Ch. Merry Rose of Woolley, Ch. Mist of Woolley, Ch. Bachelor of Woolley, Sh.Ch. Lancer of Woolley.

MORETON: Mr Kirk, his wife, 'Dovey' (who showed Griffons over the last 50 years), and his mother were based at Moreton Hall and established the Moreton kennel of Golden Retrievers. Their best-known dog was Ch. Michael of Moreton, a pre-war winner with 17 CCs, and a famous

Ch. Michael of Moreton (1936): Winner of seventeen CCs and an influential sire.

Thomas Fall.

sire. He stood at a stud fee of 25 guineas in the early 1930s – a tremendous amount for those days. Other dogs bred or shown under the Moreton affix include: Ch. Haulstone Dusty, Ch. Abbots Winkle, Ch. Mary of Moreton and Ch. Abbots Trust.

YELME: This was one of the few kennels that was a success pre and post the Second World War; it was owned by Major and Mrs Wentworth-Smith. Pre-war they owned the great sire, Gilder. They also owned and bred Ch. Cubstone Bess, Ch. Gaiety Girl of Yelme and Ch. Chief of Yelme.

Ch. Ulvin Vintage of Yelme.

ANNINGSLEY: This kennel, owned by the Venables-Kyrkes, was well-known for its winners and workers, notably Dual Ch. Anningsley Stingo. The Anningsley bloodlines were carried on after the Second World War by others, and at a time when other lines were dying out. They owned or bred Ch. Anningsley Beatrice, Ch. A. Fox and F.T. Ch. A. Crakers.

STUBBINGS: This kennel also spanned the war years. Their only home-bred pre-war Champion was Ch. Stubbings Golden Gloria, born 17.2.1931, but others were unlucky not to gain their titles. The kennel was founded when Mrs Nancy Nairn, recently settled at Stubbings Vicarage, decided to acquire a dog of a large breed as more in keeping with her surroundings. The result was Stubbings Lorelei, who was for the next twelve and a half years Mrs Nairn's devoted companion, and foundation of the kennel.

She was a great believer in the dual purpose Golden Retrievers, and at one time Stubbings housed as many as fifty dogs. Mrs Nairn died in 1942 and the kennel was carried on by her daughter, Mrs Sylvia Winston. The 'war babies', Stubbing Golden Timothy, Stubbing Golden Lalage, Stubbings Golden Nicholas, Dandylyon and Daemen, bred on and provided an important link into the lines of the late forties and fifties.

TORRDALE: This kennel started with the beautiful Ch. Dukeries Dancing Lady, born 10.7.1934. The story of the Torrdales is related by Fred Parsons (*Our Dogs* 15.11.1957):

"My wife had lost a beautiful Golden Retriever dog, Dukeries Danny Boy, a great favourite

Ch. Donkelve Rusty, 1937.

Thomas Fall.

which we mourned for quite a long time. Wishing to replace him, we travelled the whole of one Sunday (we couldn't find the way to the beautiful village of Abbots Morton), and arrived just before dark to see the litter that Mr Jenner, owner of the famous Abbot's Golden Retrievers, had advertised.

"There were only two bitch puppies in the puppy pen. I tried to persuade my wife to have the darker one, if Mr Jenner would sell, but she was determined that the lighter one was her choice if she could buy her, which she did. Mr Jenner said he had the feeling she would prove to be the best he had ever bred."

He was right in his assessment – this bitch proved to be outstanding, and she became Ch. Dukeries Dancing Lady. The Parsons went on to breed or own Ch. Donkelve Rusty, Ch. Torrdale Betty, and Sh.Ch. Torrdale Judy. This was one of the few kennels who came back after the war with an important sire, Ch. Torrdale Happy Lad; and Ch. Torrdale Faithful, Sh.Ch. Torrdale Kim of Stenbury, and Sh.Ch. Torrdale Maida followed.

DORCAS: This was possibly the most influential kennel linking pre-war and post-year breeding. In 1932 Mrs Elma Stonex bought her foundation bitch, Sally of Perrot, who won one CC. However, as a brood she wrote her name in breed history. Her son, the great stud force Dorcas Bruin, would have been a Champion except for the war. Sally's descendants went on post-war to found important new kennels.

WORKING KENNELS
Prior to 1946, no one working kennel dominated the scene. At this stage, they were dual purpose. Interestingly, the first Retriever with "Golden Retriever" relatives to win at a trial was Mr A.T. Williams' Don Of Gerwy, born in 1899. He was registered as a liver flatcoat, and he won the IGL Open Retriever Stake in 1904. His sire is given as Lord Tweedmouth's Golden flatcoat, Lucife;, his dam was Rust, a liver-coated flatcoat.

FT. Ch. Balcombe Boy was also a Show Champion, and was thus the breed's first Dual

*Sh.Ch. Torrdale
Kim of
Stenbury, 1948.*

Thomas Fall.

Champion. FT. Ch. John of Auchencheyne and FT. Ch. Eredine Rufus followed. The Venables-Kyrkes' FT. Ch. Anningsley Crackers gained his title, and they established a fine record using Crackers at stud. This included: FT. Ch. Avishays Lulu, also handled by Mr Venables-Kyrke, her son, FT. Ch. Avishays Brush, their own Dual Champion Anningsley Stingo, and Ch. Anningsley Fox. Anningsley bloodlines played an important part in the reformation of the breed after the Second World War.

Mr Eccles of the Haulstone kennel was keenly interested in the working side of the breed. In 1928 he took a step many considered regrettable when he mated Haulstone Rusty, the litter sister of Ch. Haulstone Dan, with the Yellow Labrador, FT. Ch. Haylers Defender (which was allowed at that time) with the idea of improving style and pace. An interbred daughter of the mating was put to Call Boy of Woolley, and FT. Ch. Haulstone Bob and Haulstone Lizzie were registered as Retrievers interbred.

Haulstone Lark, son of Lizzie, was mated to the pure Golden, Haulstone Gypsy, and their son, FT. Ch. Haulstone Larry was registered as a pure Golden Retriever. Larry created something of a sensation by becoming the first Golden to win the Retriever Championship. How much was due to his Labrador lines we shall never know. Since then other Golden Retrievers, without interbred blood, have won the Championship. The Eccles also owned and bred FT. Ch. Haulstone Brock. After the war they continued trialing and made up FT. Ch. Haulstone Bobby and FT. Ch. Haulstone Meg.

THE POST-WAR ERA

There were no Championship shows and no Field Trials from 1939-1946. There was little food, no time, and until the war was over, dogs had to be put to one side. Some kennels were disbanded and were never seen again. Fortunately, a few breeders kept a nucleus of stock. Following the war, there was a great demand for Golden puppies, but because dog showing had virtually come to a standstill there was no standard to judge the adults. The result was lot of very unsuitable puppies of very different types and it took quite a time to raise the standard.

DORCAS: This pre-war kennel, owned by Elma Stonex, played a leading role in reviving the breed's fortunes after the war. She was very clever breeder who, over the years, has tended to be remembered only as the breed historian. The war baby, Dorcas Bruin, winner of a Reserve CC and Junior Warrant in 1939, is remembered through his influential sons, Ch. Dorcas Glorious of Slat and Dorcas Timberscombe Topper (two CCs), and his daughters, Dorcas Felecia and Timberscombe Tansy. There was also Ch. Dorcas Gardenia, and many years later, in the 1960s, Elma Stonex won two CCs with Dorcas Octavia. Dorcas provided the foundation for some of the most influential of kennels.

TORRDALE; This was another well-known pre-war kennel which continued post-war. At eleven years of age Ch. Dukeries Dancing Lady produced two puppies, sired by her grandson, Torrdale Sandy Boy. One of the puppies died, the other became Ch. Torrdale Happy Lad, the first post-war Best in Show all breeds winner, who went on to become an important sire. The Torrdales provided foundation bitches for many kennels, plus the dog, Sh.Ch. Torrdale Kim of Stenbury, who was a link in the Stenbury kennel's breeding. They bred also Ch. Torrdale Faithful and Sh.Ch. Torrdale Maida.

ELSIVILLE: This kennel was very much 'of the Torrdale school'. It was owned by Mrs Elsie Ford, who had a lot of success in the late 1940s with Ch. Alexander of Elsiville, Sh.Ch. Nyda of Elsiville, Ch. Nikolai of Elsiville, Sh.Ch. Ophelia of Elsiville, Sh.Ch. Major of Elsiville, Sh.Ch. Shula of Elsiville and Sh.Ch. Sonja of Elsiville. In the early fifties the Fords seemed to have given up their interest in the breed. By a strange coincidence, in the late fifties my husband went to the theatre in Coventry, sand sitting in front of him was a lady wearing a huge hat. He asked, politely if she could she remove it – and he found it was Elsie Ford!

ALRESFORD: Ch. Alexander of Elsiville sired Lottie Pilkington's Ch. Alresford Advertiser, who won thirty-five CCs and was an influential sire. He was out of her lovely Ch. Alresford Mall. Lottie had some lovely Golden Retrievers pre-war, and I remember staying at her home outside Colchester and seeing all the pictures of her pre-war dogs. Post-war, following on from Mall and Advertiser, was Ch. Alresford Atom, Sh.Ch. Am. Ch. Alresford Harringay, owned by Lottie's daughter, Mrs Rampling, and finally, Sh.Ch. Alresford Purgold Tartan.

STUBBLESDOWN: This kennel, owned by Bill and Olive Hickmott, had bred and worked Golden Retrievers before the war, but they did not start showing and trialling until 1947. Two bitches, bred by Mr Jessamy, achieved fame for Stubblesdown. They were Ch. Braconlea Gaiety, a great winner including Best in Show at the Three Counties Championship Show, and Dual Champion Stubblesdown Golden Lass, who founded a Field Trial dynasty. Other notable dogs were FT. Ch. Stubblesdown Larry and FT. Ch. Westhyde Stubblesdown Major. In the mid-sixties Stubblesdown bred Ch. Stubblesdown Jester of Steddles.

ROSECOTT: The first CC winner at the first post-war Championship Show was owned by Rosemary Clark. This dog became Sh.Ch. Roger of Rosecott, and he sired the important Ch. Colin of Rosecott, a dog who excelled in stifles, which he also passed on to his progeny – many of which became Champions. Ch. Shadow of Rosecott later made her mark for the kennel.

YELME: Major Wentworth-Smith died in 1946, but Mrs Wentworth-Smith carried on the kennel and bred or showed Ch. Dernar of Yelme, Ch. Lakol of Yelme, Ch. Fillip of Yelme, and finally, Ch. Ulvin Vintage of Yelme. I remember going to my first Golden Retriever Club Championship Show at Sandford on Thames and being much in awe of Mrs Wentworth-Smith.

STENBURY: This kennel started pre-war, and in 1947 Mrs Minter made up Sh.Ch. Torrdale Kim of Stenbury. Mrs Minter's bitch line and her breeding was to become famous with Ch. Gaiety Girl of Stenbury, Ch. Charming of Stenbury, Sh.Ch. Waterwitch of Stenbury (BIS winner Championship shows), and her daughter, Sh.Ch. Watersprite of Stenbury, who was also a BIS winner at a Championship show. The late fifties saw the successful Sh.Ch. Waterwitchery of Stenbury, followed in the the early sixties by Sh.Ch. Watersonnet of Stenbury, Sh.Ch. Glennessa Waterwisp of Stenbury and Ch. Glenessa Seasprite of Stenbury. In the early seventies Ch. Nomis Portia of Stenbury made her mark along with her daughters, Sh.Ch. Stenbury Seasonnet, Sh.Ch. Stenbury Sea Laughter, and Sh.Ch. Stenbury Sea O'Dreams, her son, Ch. Stenbury Sea Tristram of Camrose. Seasonnet's daughter was Sh.Ch. Stenbury Sealace.

Mrs Minter's lovely bitch line produced the same lovely type from 1946 up to the present time. Always beautifully prepared and handled, nowadays the same line is shown in Sweden and Denmark, although Mrs Minter does not show much in the UK.

BOLTBY: Mrs Minter helped Mrs Harrison of the Boltby Golden Retriever with her breeding lines. This kennel had shown before the war, but with limited success. The turning point was the lovely Boltby Kymba (two CCs) bred by Davie Barwise (Beauchasse), sired by Sh.Ch. Torrdale Kim of Stenbury out of Dorcas Leola. Mated to the all-Torrdale-bred Boltby Sunshine and Boltby Sweet Melody, the result were the great winners and producers Ch. Boltby Skylon and Ch. Boltby Moonraker. I remember seeing Skylon win many of his CCs.

Other successful Goldens were Ch. Boltby Annabel, who also became an American Champion,

Ch. Boltby Moonraker, 1952.

Thomas Fall.

Ch. Boltby Felicity of Briarford, 1965.

Thomas Fall.

Ch. Boltby Mystral, Sh.Ch. Boltby Sugar Bush, her brother, Sh.Ch. Boltby Syrian, and the last two Boltby Champions, born 1962, Ch. Boltby Felicity of Briarford and her brother Ch. Irish Ch. Cabus Boltby Combine.

BEAUCHASSE: Davie Barwise was a teacher who lived in Wigton. His foundation bitch, Dorcas Leola, produced Sh.Ch. Beauchasse Bergamat, who produced Ch. Beauchasse Dominie. Dominie was sire of Ch. Beauchasse Gaiety, foundation of Jean Burnett's Fordvales and Rossbournes. The last title holder for Beauchasse was Sh.Ch. Beauchasse Nous, born 19.12.1959. However, Beauchasse Jason (one CC) was the sire of a very important stud dog of the sixties, Champion and Irish Champion Cabus Cadet. Beauchasse also bred Boltby Kymba, an important sire for the Boltby kennel.

YEO: This, along with Westley, is one of the two kennels post-war that has bred Field Trial Champions and Champions. Mrs Lucille Sawtell's home-bred Ch. Masterpiece of Yeo was born in 1942 and carried on the Anningsley bloodlines (he was sired by Ch. Anningsley Fox). Masterpiece took his title in 1951 at nine years of age. His daughter became FT. Ch. Musicmaker of Yeo. Sh. Ch. Pandown Poppet of Yeo, born 12.5.1954, was from Torrdale/Beauchasse bloodlines. Poppet's son, Ringmaster of Yeo, was an important stud force. He was sire of Champion and American Champion Figaro of Yeo. Another FT. Ch., Holway Flush of Yeo, was bred here. Figaro mated to his grandmother, Poppet, threw Sh.Ch. Halsham Hifi of Yeo. Another Ringmaster son was Ch. Toddytavern Kummel of Yeo.

In the early sixties Mrs Sawtell owned, in partnership with Mrs Harkness from Ireland, Ch. & Irish Ch. Mandingo Buidhe Colum. The first time I awarded Challenge Certificates in Golden Retrievers in the sixties, Column won the dog CC. One of the loveliest bitches was Ch. Deerflite Endeavour of Yeo. Her son was Sh.Ch. Concord of Yeo who was sire of Sh.Ch. Trident of Yeo

Ch. Deerflite
Endeavour of Yeo.

Colbar. Concord's sister, Caravelle, produced Ch. Challenger of Yeo Glengilde, and another sister, Caprice, was dam of the good stud dog, Ch. Moorquest Mugwump. Yeo has been a most important kennel for the breed.

DEERFLITE: Liz Borrow's kennel has been important for its bloodlines. Starting with a Dorcas foundation bitch, Aurora mated to Ch. Torrdale Happy produced Sh.Ch. Sonnet, born 5.2.1949. A very typical Golden, Sonnet was the sire of Ch. Deerflite Delilah, and for his owners he also sired Ch. Avondale Brandy. Brandy and Delilah (half-brother and sister) produced Ch. Deerflite Headline. Headline's daughter, Deerflite Highlight, produced Sh.Ch. Deerflite Rainfall, who was the dam of the lovely Ch. Deerflite Endeavour of Yeo. A repeat of Endeavour's mating produced Sh.Ch. Deerflite Paragon. Rainfall's son, Deerflite Tradition of Janville, sired Ch. Moorquest Mugwump. Therefore, the Deerflite line is found in many South-Western pedigrees also through Endeavour's Yeo litters.

ANBRIA: This kennel, so well-known in Margaret Barron's lifetime, is now seemingly only remembered for having bred the sire of the great Ch. Camrose Cabus Christopher. Always beautifully dressed, Margaret Barron was kind to everybody; her dogs were always beautifully put down and handled. She started with two dogs from Mrs Wills. The dog was Sh.Ch. Anbria Andrew of Arbrook, and her foundation bitch, Ch. Briar of Arbrook. Briar was the dam of Ch. Jane of Anbria, who was the dam of Ch. Miranda of Anbria. Ch. Jane also produced the good sire, Ch. Camrose Tallyrand of Anbria. Ch. Miranda was granddam of Ch. Melody of Anbria and dam of Sh.Ch. Anbria Laudable. Tallyrand sired Sh.Ch. Anbria Tantalus. Mrs Clark, famous for her Joriemour Griffons, bred two Anbria Champions out of Anbria Stock, namely Ch. Anbria Joriemour Marigold and Ch. Anbria Schumac. I had a daughter of Ch. Briar Noreen of Anbria, but she did not really like showing, so she did not emulate her famous kennelmates.

Sh. Ch. Stolford Joy.

STOLFORD: Mrs Peggy Robertson's kennel came to the fore in the mid-fifties with Sh.Ch. Stolford Joy, bred from the Breckland's bloodlines which also lie behind the successful sire, Ch. and Irish Ch. Cabus Cadet. In the sixties came the brother and sister, Sh.Ch. Stolford Samala and Sh.Ch. Samdor Stolford Samarkand (a BIS winner at a general Championship Show), followed by Samarkand's daughter, Sh.Ch. Stolford Jasmine. Samala's grandson was the great show and stud dog, Ch. Stolford Happy Lad. Happy Lad's daughter was Ch. Stolford Merienda, who shared the same breeding as Ch. Stolford Sheralee of Talleego. His two sons were Sh.Ch. and NZ Ch. Happy Chance of Stolford and Sh.Ch. Stolford Likely Lad.

GLENNESSA: This kennel, owned by Wing Cdr. Iles and his wife, Muriel, has been the foundation for many southern kennels. I remember their big winner in the fifties, Glennessa Alexa. In the sixties they came to the fore with Alexa's granddaughters, Ch. Glennessa Seasprite of Stenbury and Ch. Glennessa Seashanta, Alexa's great grandson, Sh.Ch. Glennessa Leaderman, Sh.Ch. Glennessa Emma of Fivewinds, Emma's daughter, Sh.Ch. Glennessa Petrushka, and her daughter,Sh. Ch. Glennessa Clare. Bred by Mrs Minter, Sh. Ch. Glennessa Waterwisp of Stenbury completes some of their titled stock.

THE SIXTIES AND SEVENTIES

JANVILLE: Mrs J.E. Harrison (no relation to Mrs 'Boltby' Harrison) has provided influential lines for other kennels, especially through her home-bred Sh.Ch. Janville Renown. A winner of many CCs, Ch. Cabus Janville Defender sired some important progeny. Mrs Harrison also bred Sh.Ch. Janville Yorkist and Sh.Ch. Janville Tempestuous at Lincheal.

CABUS: Mr and Mrs Moriaty, now Mrs Morgan, of the Cabus prefix is famous for its stud dogs – and they seemed to prefer showing dogs to bitches, although I remember them showing Sh.Ch. Boltby Sugar Bush for Mrs Harrison. They bred Int. Ch. Cabus Cadet and owned his sons, Int. Ch. Cabus Boltby Combine and Ch. Cabus Janville Defender. They mated their Cadet daughter, Cabus Boltby Charmer, to Ch. Camrose Tallyrand of Anbria and produced the top sire (who still holds

Styal Snowflake of Remington, pictured as a youngster.

David Bull.

that record today) and a longtime breed CC record holder, Ch. Camrose Cabus Christopher. An earlier litter had included Ch. Cabus Caruso and Ch. Hughenden Cabus Columbia.

STYAL: Mrs Hazel Hinks kept Golden Retrievers before she started to show. Ch. Styal Sibella, born 21.12.1965, was the dam of Ch. Styal Susila, an important brood bitch. Susila produced the 'Poets' litter: Ch. Styal Shakespeare and Sh. Ch. Styal Shelley of Maundale, Ch. Styal Scott of Glengilde (CC record holder), and her own Sh. Ch. Styal Symetrya. Using Sibella, Mrs Hinks also bred Ch. Styal Stefanie of Camrose, the breed record holder in bitches with twenty-seven CCs. Styal has provided many kennels with good foundations.

GYRIMA: The late Marigold Timpson started with two bitches – Styal Sonnet of Gyrima and Sh.Ch. Romside Raffeena. Sonnet produced three title holders: Ch. Gyrima Pippaline, Ch. G. Pipparanda and Ch. G. Pipparetta. Pippaline, foundation of the Ninell kennel, was the dam of Ch. Ninell Crusade of Dabess; Sh.Ch. Ninell Charade of Nortonwood, granddam of Ch. Ninell Franchesca, who was dam of Ch. Ninell Morwenna, who was herself dam of Ch. Ninell Rambruen. Ch. Gyrima Pipparanda was the first title holder for Dr and Mrs A. Morris (Sandusky), who also bred, in partnership with Mrs Day, Sh.Ch. Sandusky Brigitta of Darris and her son, Ch. Darris Double Diamond. After Marigold Timpson's untimely death, they took Gyrima Solitaire and won the two CCs needed to complete her title. Gyrima made up the third title holder, Sh.Ch. Gyrima Pipparetta, who was dam of the lovely Sh.Ch. Gyrima Moonstone, who was herself dam of Sh.Ch. Gyrima Wystonia of Camrose.

   The other Gyrima foundation bitch, Sh.Ch. Romside Raffeena of Gyrima, born 13.1.1966, was the dam of Sh.Ch. Gyrima Ariadne. Raffeena was granddam of Sh.Ch. Gyrima Oliver, who was sire of Sh.Ch. Portcullis Greeting of Gyrima.

DAVERN: I have known Chas and Brenda Lowe for as long as I have been involved with dogs, and over the years they have had some outstanding Golden Retrievers. In the sixties they made up Ch. Sutton Rudy. Then came Ch. Camrose Pruella of Davern (BIS at a general Championship Show), Ch. Davern Figaro, Mrs Beck's lovely Sh.Ch. Davern Josephine, winner of eighteen CCs,

Ch. Davern Figaro, 1981.

Sh.Ch. Davern Rosabella, Sh.Ch. Verdayne Dandini of Davern, Sh.Ch. Davern Alpine Rose of Lacons and Sh. Ch. Amirene King Eider of Davern.

TEECON: This kennel enjoyed considerable success in the sixties and seventies. The Tirantis had Sh.Ch. Gamebird Debonair of Teecon, Sh.Ch. Peatling Stella of Teecon, Ch. Teecon Ambassador and Sh.Ch. Teecon Knight Errant – then the Teecon prefix was never used again. Mr Tiranti and Mrs Janet Tiranti have used the GARTHFIELD affix for about fourteen years, making up Sh.Ch. Pitcote Arcadian of Garthfield. Mrs Pat Holmes, formerly Mrs Tiranti, has, in partnership with Bill Holmes, used the BEACONHOLM affix, making up Sh.Ch. Elzac Amber of Beaconholm.

LEADING KENNELS

MELFRICKA: This Midlands-based kennel, owned by Mrs and Mrs Hathaway, has been showing since the early seventies. Successes include: Sh.Ch. Lindys Butterscotch of Melfricka, Sh.Ch. Melfricka Echo, Sh Ch. Melfricka Kudos of Rossbourne, Sh.Ch. Melfricka Zed, Sh.Ch. Melfricka Love Story, and Ob. Ch. Melfricka Limelight.

Sh.Ch.
Melfricka Echo.

David Dalton.

ROSSBOURNE: Before her marriage Jean Burnett's Fordvale dogs were well-known. Her foundation bitch was Ch. Beauchasse Gaiety, dam of Ch. Fordvale Gay Moonlynn. Then came Sh.Ch. Rossbourne Timothy, his son and Sh.Ch. Rossbourne Harvest Gold, Sh.Ch. Rossbourne Abbotsford Hope, Sh.Ch. Rossbourne In Love and Sh.Ch. Melfricka Kudos of Rossbourne.

Sh. Ch. Janville Temptestuous at Linchael: The first in a long line of title-winners for the Linchael kennel.

LINCHAEL: This highly successful northern kennel is owned by Mrs Lyn Anderson, who started in the breed in 1965. Lyn has written a book, in which she highlights the many setbacks she endured, but,with determination, she battled on, never giving up. Sh.Ch. Janville Tempestuous At Linchael, born 24.6.1974, was her first title holder. Then came Tempestuous's daughter, Sh.Ch. Linchael Heritage, followed by Heritage's half-brother, Sh.Ch. Linchael Excelsior. Lyn's other bitch line produced Sh.Ch. Linchael Delmoss, Sh.Ch. Linchael Freya of Gloi, Sh.Ch. Linchael Cartier of Gloi, then Ch. Linchael Wild Silk and brother, Sh.Ch. Linchael Conspiracy of Chevanne. For two years Lyn had the Norwegian Ch. Mjaerumhogdas Crusader (one CC) at stud in the UK. At the beginning of the year at a Club Championship Show, I gave the all Norwegian-bred Linchael Gullviva the CC – I thought she was an excellent bitch. Now the Linchaels are almost into their twenty-ninth year in Goldens, hopefully with as much pleasure and success to look forward to.

NORTONWOOD: I have known Ron and Madge Bradbury of the Nortonwoods for more years than I care to remember, and although they have made up bitches, they are known worldwide for their famous stud dogs. Ch. Nortonwood Faunus, born 15.2.1974, was, like his sire, Christopher, a great stud dog. He sired nineteen British title holders and won thirteen CCs. Other influential sires include: Sh.Ch. Westley Munro of Nortonwood, Sh.Ch. Nortonwood Checkmate, and Sh.Ch. Nortonwood Silvanus. The bitches that have been made up are Sh.Ch. Nortonwood Canella, Sh.Ch. Ninell Charade of Nortonwood, plus Westley Sabrina of Nortonwood and Amirene Egretta of Nortonwood with two CCs each. The latest star, with eleven CCs and a Reserve BIS at a Championship Show to date, is the Silvanus son, Sh.Ch. Jobeka Jasper of Nortonwood, who has already produced some promising progeny.

SANSUE: Mrs Val Birkin has produced a great line of sires and lovely bitches, starting with Tingel Concorde, born in 1964. Then came the great sire and show dog, Ch. Sansue Camrose Phoenix. I remember giving him one of his early CCs – he won fourteen in all. He sired Ch. Westley Victoria, the brood bitch record holder. Then came the following British title holders: Ch.

Sh.Ch. Jobeka Jasper of Nortonwood: The latest star of the Nortonwood kennel.

David Dalton.

Ch. Moonsprite Mermaid of Carasan: The top Golden Retriever in the UK in 1990.

David Bull.

Sansue Saracen of Westley, Sh.Ch. Milo Hollybush of Sansue, Ch. Sansue Tobias, Ch. Westley Topic of Sansue, Ch. Sansue Cressida of Manoan, Sh.Ch. Sansue Wrainbow, Ch. Gaineda Consolidator of Sansue, Ch. Sansue Pepper of Lovhayne, Sh.Ch. Sansue Phoebe, Ch. Sansue Golden Ruler, Ch. Sansue Royal Fancy, Ch. Sansue Royal Flair, Ch. Sansue Spring Mist of Rambleyne, and finally, Ch. Sansue Xtra Polite. Sandra Birkin has joined her mother with Sansue – so the best of luck with the next thirty years.

KENNELS OF SPECIAL SIGNIFICANCE

The Westley and Camrose kennels are the most important the breed has known since 1946. It would be hard to find any show winner, of whatever strain, without a Westley or a Camrose dog somewhere in their five-generation pedigree.

*Ch. Clarissa of
Westley.*

*Sally Anne
Thompson.*

*Sh.Ch. Westley
Simone: winner
of twelve CCs.*

David Dalton.

WESTLEY

Joan Gill started her kennel pre-war with Simon of Brookshill (Stubbings/Abbots breeding), who was given to her in 1936 as a birthday present. He was a big, pale dog, with a beautifully chiselled head. Major Wentworth-Smith admired him and used him on his own bitch, Lively of Yelme; Joan had Westley Frolic of Yelme from the mating. She was to become the dam of the influential stud and show dog, Ch. Simon of Westley (twenty-one CCs, 1st and other Field Trial awards), the lovely Ch. Sally of Westley, and Ch. Kolahoi Willow of Westley. Pre-war Joan also bought Speedwell Dulcet. This bitch played no part in the Westley story, but was great grandmother of FT. Ch. Treunair Cala.

Post-war, on Major Wentworth-Smith's advice, Joan bought from Miss Dixon a Ch. Hazelgilt granddaughter. She became Ch. Susan of Westley, dam of another important sire, Ch. William of Westley, whose name is in many pedigrees. Susan was also dam of an 'only', the only Dual Champion and Irish Dual Champion in the breed, David of Westley, owned by Miss L. Ross, trained by Mr J. Cranston. William and Sally produced Sh.Ch. Annette of Westley, then William, as an old dog, sired Ch. Camrose Nicolas of Westley. 'Nicky' was an important stud dog and winner of twenty CCs, a Field Trial winner, and BIS at a general Championship Show. I remember the party after Nicky's BIS at Joan Tudors – we all drank champagne out of the BIS cup! Nicky was a fantastic character, once known never forgotten, but I think Ch. Simon was Joan's once-in-a-lifetime dog.

A rare achievement followed. Echo, a show-bred bitch (although Westley were dual-purpose) produced FT. Ch. Holway Teal of Westley. In 1968 Echo whelped Ch. Pippa of Westley, winner of seventeen CCs. She was a lovely bitch – I gave her a CC in Scotland when Phoenix won the dog CC. Then Joan Gill and Daphne Philpott went into partnership, and stage two of the Westley story followed, with Daphne and her husband, Mervyn, adding their expertise and knowledge. Ch. Sansue Saracan of Westley was followed by the superb Ch. Clarissa of Westley. In 1970 a Pippa granddaughter was produced. This was Ch. Westley Jacquetta, a lovely bitch, a winner at trials, and dam of Ch. Westley Victoria. She was the top brood bitch in the breed, dam of Sh.Ch. Westley Tartan of Buidhe, Ch. Westley Topic of Sansue, Sh.Ch. Westley Munro of Nortonwood, Ch. Westley Mabella (twenty-two CCs), Ch. Westley Martha, Sh.Ch. Westley Simone (twelve CCs), Ch. Westley Samual and Sh.Ch. Westley Sophia of Papeta. Mabella produced Ch. Westley Felicia of Siatham and Sh.Ch. Westley Jacob. Martha produced Ch. Westley Ramona, the Standfast foundation bitch. Jacob's sister, Julianna, produced Sh.Ch. Westley Clementina and Sh.Ch. Westley Christina.

The Westley story does not finish there. Daphne has the Standerwick prefix for Field Trial lines, and she has enjoyed tremendous success. The current tally stands at twenty-seven British Westley title holders plus five British Standerwick G.B. FT. Ch. title holders – that is certainly a hard act to follow!

CAMROSE

Mrs Joan Tudor's foundation was a well-bred bitch, born in 1946. Golden Camrose Tess won one CC and one Reserve CC, but through her descendants she has written her name in the history of the breed. She is the dam of Ch. Camrose Anthea, and of the first great Camrose stud dog, Ch. Camrose Fantango, who sired Ch. Camrose Tantara, Sh.Ch. Broadwaters Camrose Tangay, and Ch. Camrose Jessica who was the dam of Ch. Camrose Nicolas of Westley. Tantara was the dam of

Ch. Camrose Cabus Christopher: The great British sire with a tally of twenty-six title holders in the UK to his name.

Diane Pearce.

a great favourite of mine, Ch. Camrose Lucius, and his sister, Ch. Camrose Loretta, who, I think, could win today. Lucius's daughter was Ch. Camrose Tamarisk.

Another great stud dog sired by Fantango was Ch. Camrose Tallyrand of Anbria, winner of sixteen CCs. He sired Loretta's daughter, Ch. Camrose Wistura, Ch. Camrose Gay Delight of Sladeham, and Loretta had three titled grandchildren, Ch. Camrose Pruella of Davern, Sh.Ch. Camrose Psyche of Vementry and Ch. Sansue Camrose Phoenix. The immortal Ch. Camrose Cabus Christopher (sired by Tallyrand, was the top sire with twenty-six title holders, also the one-time breed record holder with forty-one CCs), Ch. Berm. Can. Ch. Camrose Evenpatrol – a much travelled dog. For quite a few years the Camrose kennel was owned in partnership with Miss Rosemary Wilcock, and their combined successes included: Sh.Ch. Camrose Matilda, Ch. Styal Stefanie of Camrose, bitch breed record holder with twenty-seven CCs, and Sh.Ch. Camrose Hardangerfjord of Beldonburn, and another top stud was Ch. Camrose Fabius Tarquin (twenty CCs), plus Ch. Stenbury Sea Tristram of Camrose, Sh.Ch. Gyrima Wystonia of Camrose, Ch. Camrose Waterlyric of Beldonburn, and Sh.Ch. Camrose Frangipani of Beldonburn. In Mrs Tudor's ownership is Sh.Ch. Camrose Tulfes Intirol.

POST-WAR FIELD TRIAL KENNELS

HOLWAY

Unlike the pre-war Field Trial scene, the post war era has been dominated by one kennel, Holway, and its handlers Mrs June Atkinson, her late husband, Martin, and now her son, Robert. Holway is the connecting thread throughout the Golden Retriever Field Trial world. In 1954 FT. Ch. Mazurka of Wynford won the Retriever Championship with June Atkinson. This was followed twenty-eight

June Atkinson and Ft. Ch. Holway Dollar pictured in the line at a Field Trial.

Graham Cox.

*Ch. Standerwick
Thomasina
bringing a cock
pheasant to hand
through the snow.*

G. Cox.

years later by her son winning the Championship with FT. Ch. Little Marston Chorus of Holway. June Atkinson has a record as a breeder, trainer and handler of Golden Retrievers which cannot be equalled by any other retriever breed.

Her FT Champion list is as follows: Musicmaker of Yeo, Mazurka of Wynford, Holway Zest, Holway Bonnie, Holway Lancer, Holway Flush of Yeo, Holway Teal of Westley, Palgrave Holway Harmony, Holway Westhyde Zeus, Palgrave Holway Folly, Holway Gaiety, Holway Barrister, Holway Jollity, Holway Spinner, Holway Gorse, Holway Chanter, Holway Gem, Holway Calla, L.M. Chorus of Holway, Holway Dollar, Holway Trumpet, Holway Grettle, Holway Eppie, Holway Denier, Holway Corbiere, Holway Ruby and Holway Crosa.

STUBBLESDOWN: This kennel made up a Dual Championship in Stubblesdown Golden Lass, then FT. Ch. Stubblesdown Larry, FT. Ch. Westhyde Stubblesdown Major.

WESTYHYDE: Mrs P. Fraser had a lot of success, especially with the 'Z' litter – FT. Champions Westhyde Zurka, Zeus and Zenith.

PALGRAVE: The brilliant trainer Eric Baldwin had success with either handling or breeding FT. Champions Holway Teal of Westley, Palgrave Holway Harmony, Palgrave Holway Folly, Palgrave Fern of Ardyle, Volvo of Palgrave.

TREUNAIR: Mrs J. Lumsden's FT. Ch. Treunair Cala was winner of the 1952 Retriever Championships. Other successes include: FT. Ch. Treunair Texa, FT. Ch. Treunair Strathcarron Alexa, and FT. Ch. Treunair Kelso.

STANDERWICK: In the seventies, Daphne Philpot become interested in training for the field. Buying from Miss McRae Strathcarron Seil of Standerwick, Daphne produced a line that not only she, an excellent trainer, could train on, but others also. Seil mated to FT. Ch. Holway Spinner produced a bitch, Ch. Standerwick Thomasina, who only just missed being a Dual Champion. When Seil was mated to Belway Flick of Flight line, the result was Mrs W. Andrew's FT. Ch. Standerwick Rumbustuous of Catcombe, and Mr R. Burn's FT. Ch. Standerwick Roberta of Abnalls, an award winner in the Retriever Championship. Seil's granddaughter was FT. Ch. Standerwick Donna of Deadcroft.

However, the greatest achievement of all for Daphne was when she handled Roberta's daughter, FT. Ch. Abnalls Hilary of Standerwick, to her title.

OBEDIENCE CHAMPIONS
The first Golden Retriever Obedience Champion was Ob. Ch. Castelnau Pizzicato, who won in the show ring as well. He was born in 1956, sired by Ch. Camrose Fantago. Ob. Ch. Nicholas of Albesden was by Ch. Camrose Tallyrand of Anbria, Ob. Ch. Nana of Bournemouth was by Sh.Ch. Anbria Tantalus, and Ob. Ch. Golden Seeker was out of Leygore Juno. The handsome Ob. Ch. Melfricka Limelight was by Ch. Camrose Fabius Tarquin, and Ob. Ch. Kingsley Golden Lass was by Temevale Foxtrot of Empshott.

NORTHERN IRELAND
Northern Ireland can lay claim to one of the most famous Golden Retrievers as a resident. Int. Dual Ch. David of Westley (Ch. Dorcas Glorious of Slat – Ch. Susan of Westley) was born on June 6th 1951, bred by Joan Gill, owned by Lucy Ross of County Down. She also bought Stubblesdown Vanda, who became an Irish FT.Ch. When mated to David, Vanda produced Buidhe Derag, who when mated to Alresford Nice Fella produced Ch. Ir.Ch. Mandingo Buidhe Colum, owned by Mrs E. Harkness and Mrs L. Sawtell. Miss Ross also owned and campaigned English Sh.Ch. Westley Tartan of Buidhe.

The most influential kennel in Northern Ireland has been Eva Harkness's kennel, which was started in 1955. She brought over from England Alresford Nice Fella in 1962. Nice Fella's matings to Lucky Charm of Yeo provided the Mandingo foundation stock. The first litter included Ir. Ch. Mandingo Marianne, and her sister Marigold, foundation of Heather Avis' Glenavis kennel. Marigold was an Irish Ch. and won two CCs in England. She was the dam of Eng. Sh.Ch. Norwegian Ch. Glenavis Barman.

The second mating of Alresford Nice Fella and Lucky Charm of Yeo produced Eng. Sh.Ch. Ir. Ch Mandingo Beau Ideal, Mandingo Beau Geste of Yeo, sire of Champions in Britain. There have been many more Mandingo winners up to the present time. When in Northern Ireland the Glenavis kennel produced many winners including: Sh Ch. Glenavis Barman, Danish Ch. Glenavis Bellagirl and S. African Ch. Glenavis Bandsman. When Heather Avis moved to Scotland she made up Eng. Ir. Ch. Mytonvale Jessica of Glenavis, a Championship Group winner.

The Seamourne kennel, owned by Mr Massey, was based on a Lygore foundation and has produced many Irish Champions. Mrs Kate Black's Lislone kennel is well-known both in Northern Ireland and England. Her outstanding dog must be Eng. Ir. Ch. Garbank Special Edition of Lislone, who is still winning CCs from the veteran class. Lislone has sent many winners to Canada and Finland. Other Northern Ireland include Avoncraig, Whitewater, Greenglen and Ruadth.

Chapter Thirteen

GOLDEN RETRIEVERS IN NORTH AMERICA

THE SHOW SCENE

EARLY HISTORY

The first photographs of a Golden Retriever in North America go back to the foundations of the breed in Great Britain. Quoting from British gentlemen in the Wild West: "In Collingsworth and Wheeler Counties, at the South Eastern corner of the Texas panhandle was a British company that although it was managed by British Aristocrats became involved with the capital intensive ranching system practiced in that state. A syndicate headed by a Scottish baron had acquired 150,400 acres of the best watered land for $1.25 per acre from Earl Winfield Spencer and Jacob John Drew. With the land came a herd of cattle and the Rocking Chair brand which lent its name to the company formed by the British. The company was formed in Great Britain in 1883 with a capital of £150,000 in three thousand shares of £50 each. The largest shareholder was the 1st Lord Tweedmouth (a man given to ungovernable rages). Also in the venture his son-in-law John Campbell Hamilton Gordon, 7th Earl of Aberdeen (later Viceroy of Ireland and Governor General of Canada for which service he was elevated to a Marquess), and his nephew, Henry Edward Fox-Strangeways 5th Earl of Ilchester."

On that first shareholders list of only fourteen names was Sir Piers Henry Cotterell and Sir John Clayton Conell, private secretary to Queen Victoria's second son, Prince Alfred Duke of Edinburgh. Lord Tweedmouth sent his youngest son, the Hon Archie Marjoribanks, then aged twenty-two, to be co-manager of the ranch. His brother, the Hon Coutts Marjoribanks caught the ranching bug, and a smaller spread (cost $30,000) was bought in Dakota territory, called the Horse Shoe ranch. He later went on to manage Gausachan, a 480 acre farm on Lake Okanagan in British Columbia.

The ranch project failed, but our interest lies in the fact that Archie Marjoribanks brought with him a Golden Retriever called Sol (Sweep – Zoe) born March 1882. Sol appears in Lord Tweedmouth's stud book, listed in 1882, 1883 and 1884, when it is noted, that he was given to Archie and later died at the ranch. In a letter I received from Lord Hailsham, he states how his mother (Archie's American-born wife) often mentioned Sol. The dog was named by Lord Tweedmouth, so he was obviously of the ideal golden colour. Archie also had a Golden Retriever bitch called Lady with him, and she is photographed in about 1894 with the Aberdeens in Canada. The bitch's name is written on the photograph, so we have proof that this was the bitch in question. After the failure of the ranch, Archie served as an aide-de-camp to his brother-in-law in Canada. Lady is not mentioned in Lord Tweedmouth's listings, probably because she went out after 1890 when the kennel record ends. However, we do know that Lady was ancestress to the foundation of the Culham kennel, so it is indeed fitting that she spent time in both Great Britain and North America, truly an international ancestress.

We have no other record of Golden Retrievers during the early 1900s, although some might have come to the East or West coast from Great Britain. The influential Gilnockie kennel was founded by Bert Armstrong in Winnipeg, Canada in 1918. Probably the man who did more for the breed in its beginnings in North America, helping to form the Golden Retriever Club of America, was Colonel S.S. Magoffin, who in 1928 founded Rockhaven kennel in British Columbia. When Bert Armstrong died, Col Magoffin acquired his Gilnockie kennel. He kept the Rockhaven kennel in British Columbia, and he established the Gilnockie at Inglewood, Colorado, where both he and his brother-in-law, Ralph Boalt, had homes.

Col Magoffin imported from Great Britain the great founding sire, Am. Can. Ch. Speedwell Pluto (Ch. Michael of Moreton – Sh. Ch. Speedwell Emerald). Born May 26th 1929, he went over to the USA, a well-broken gun dog and show winner, and became the first Golden Retriever Champion in the USA. He followed his American title with his Canadian title in 1934, and he was one of the greatest sires for both the USA and Canada. The Rockhaven bitch foundations were Saffron Chipmonk and Penelope, who were sired by Ch. Haulstore Dan out of Dame Daphne (Speedwell Nimrod – Guiding Star). Col Magoffin's Wilderness Tangerine also won both American and Canadian titles.

IMPORTANT IMPORTS

The Golden Retriever was officially recognised by the American Kennel Club in 1932. In Canada the Golden Retrievers were recognised as a separate breed and were registered by the Canadian Kennel Club in 1927. The Golden Retriever Club of Ontario was formed in 1958 and in 1960 became the Golden Retriever Club of Canada.

Colonel Magoffin was obviously trying to get the best foundation for the breed in North America. I have copies of three letters sent to him from Mrs Charlsworth (Noranby), Mrs Hextall (Avishays) and Mrs Walker (Ch. Hazelgilt) in December 1938, answering his questions. By that time Sheila Clark of Pennsylvania (1938) had imported Ch. Noranby Deirdre, in-whelp to Dual Ch. Anningsley Stings. Dr Charles Large of New York (Frantell) bought Ch. Anningsley Beatrice over, and Peter Jackson of Santa Barbara imported Ch. Marine of Woolley.

Ch. Marine of Woolley was shown but he did not complete his American title. However, he sired Am. Ch. Rockhaven Whitebridge Nobby, who was born in 1935. Mrs Cottingham (Woolley) also sent over Ch. Vesta of Woolley to Mrs Paul Moore, and this bitch also gained her American title. Another dog who held both English and American titles, Bingo of Yelme, lies behind many American pedigrees as the sire of Gilnockie Coquette, born in 1938, owned and bred by Ralph Boalt. This dog left an indelible mark on American bloodlines and on the Stilrovin prefix. Ralph Boalt's kennels were based at Winona, Minnesota.

The Cragmount kennels of Mrs C.W. Englehard is no longer in existence, but they produced so many great dogs. They bought Ch. Figaro of Yeo from Lucille Sawtell in the UK and he took his American title (1965), and did a lot of winning.

Mr Englehard had Chieftain of Yeo as his personal companion, and the dog went everywhere with him – even on his plane. Lucille Sawtell has sent quite a few Yeos to North America. Frolic of Yeo went to Mr and Mrs Beckworth of Minnesota, where she won titles and was bred from. Two other English imports, Ch. Ambassador of Davern (Shadywell) and Ch. Symbol of Yeo made the Stud Dog Hall of Fame.

Am. Can. Ber. Ch.
Cummings Gold Rush
Charlie

TOP: Pictured in his
prime as the top-winning
Golden Retriever in the
seventies and eighties.

RIGHT: Still winning
from the veteran class,
and sire of some
exceptional producers.

J. Luria.

INFLUENTIAL DOGS

Important dogs of the fifties, sixties, and seventies, who have bred on, producing other important dogs include Am. Can. Ch. Golden Knolls King Alphonzo, born in December 1949, bred by Mrs Russell Petersen and owned by A. Perry, then N.B. Ashby. King Alphonzo and his relations dominated show rings in the fifties and sixties. From King's tally of thirty-three Champion offspring, sixteen were out of Ch. Chee Chee of Sprucewood (including two who were placed in Field Trials). His line-bred grand-daughter, Ch Sprucewood's Harvest Sugar, also produced sixteen title holders and was a foundation for several modern kennels.

Ch. Sunset's Happy Duke, born in August 1964, owned and bred by Charles Cronheim, is important through the influence of his two sons, Ch. Misty Morn's Sunset CD, TD, WC and Am. Can. Ch. Cummings Gold Rush Charlie. Misty Morn's Sunset produced more than 130 Show Champions and Obedience titled dogs. Ch. Cummings Gold Rush Charlie set fantastic show records, winning Top Sporting Dog 1974, forty-three Best in Show awards and ninety-six Group wins. Charlie also produced a number of exceptional producers.

An outstanding kennel of workers was the Tigathoes of Mrs George Flinn JR of Connecticut. This prefix is also behind many bench winners, but is best-known for Field Trial Champions, Dual Champions top sires and top dams. Barbara Howard's import of AFC Holway Barty, born February 1971, from the top Holway Field Trial Kennels in the UK has had a great influence when crossed back on to American field lines.

AMERICAN TITLES

CHAMPION: Championship points can be won by one dog and one bitch in each breed. The Winners Dog and Winners Bitch receive these points. The number of points depends on the number of each sex competing in each breed. When a dog has received 15 points, two winnings of which must be three or more points, that is a Champion.

AFC or AFCh: Amateur Field Champion
BB or BOB: Best of Breed
CD: Companion Dog (lst level Obedience title)
CDX: Companion Dog Excellent (2nd level Obedience Title)
Ch: Champion (Conformation)
DCh: Dual Champion (FC and Ch).
FC or FCh: Field Champion
FDHF: Field Dog Hall of Fame (GRCA Award)
HIT or HSDT: "High in Trial" or Highest Scoring Dog in Trial
JAM: Judges Award of Merit
JH: Junior Hunter
SH: Senior Hunter
MH: Master Hunter
NAFC: National Amateur Field Champion
NFC or NFCh: National Field Trial Champion
OD: Outstanding Dam – GRCA Award
ODHF: Obedience Dog Hall of Fame – GRCA Award
OS: Outstanding Sire – GRCA Award
OTCh: Obedience Trial Champion
SDHF: Show Dog Hall of Fame – GRCA Award
TD: Tracking Dog
TDX:Tracking Dog Excellent
UD: Utility Dog (3rd level Obedience Title)
UDT: Utility Dog Tracker (UD and TD)
UDTX: Utility Dog Tracker Excellent (UD and TDX)
VC: Versatility Certificate (GRCA title)
VCX: Versatility Excellent Certificate (GRCA title)
WC: Working Certificate (GRCA title)
WCX: Working Certificate Excellent (GRCA title)
WB: Winners Bitch
WD: Winners Dog
WC: Any placement or a JAM in Derby or a 3rd or 4th placement or a JAM in a Qualifying Stake, in an AKC Licensed or Member Field Trial.

CANADIAN TITLES

To become a Canadian Champion, ten points must be won under at least three different judges. The points are awarded according to the number of dogs competing in the breed. The largest number of points obtainable at one show is five. Field Trials are similar to America, and to become a Field Champion a dog must win ten points. Five points must be won by taking first prize in an Open All Age Stake.

PRESENT-DAY KENNELS

AMBERAC

Ellen Manke, Wisconsin (North Central) has bred many Champions. She owned Am. Can. Ch. Amberac's Asterling Aruba, born in August 1979, bred by Mary Burke. This bitch has an outstanding show record; she is a Best In Show winner, and she also has an outstanding record as a brood bitch. From her five litters, more than thirty offspring have completed Championships. One of her daughters, Ch. Asterling's Tahiti Sweetie has excelled in the show ring. Aruba is line-bred to Ch. Misty Morn's Sunset CD, TD, WC.

Ch. Asterling's Tahiti Sweetie: A top winning bitch in the USA.

J. Luria.

ASTERLING

Owned by Mary Burke, Wisconsin, this kennel produced Ch. Asterling's Tahiti Sweetie, owned in partnership with Sylvia Donalay. This bitch had a fantastic show career and is in the Show Dog hall of Fame. Mary is currently campaigning the top winning Ch. Asterling's Wild Blue Yonder (Ch. Signature Sound Barrier – Ch. Asterlings Wingmaster) who has over forty-five Best in Show awards.

Ch. Asterling's Wild Blue Yonder (call name: James), whelped June 1988. This dog holds all breed records in the AKC and GRCA for conformation. To date, this includes fifty-one All Breed Best in Show, and twenty Best in Specialty Shows. James has always been breeder/owner-handled, and he is the sire of over thirty AKC Champions – and the number increases monthly.

AMBERCROFT
Owned by Carole A. Lee of Ontario, this kennel was founded on American and British bloodlines, and many Champions have come from their line.

BECKWITH
Richard and Ludell Beckwith, Washington (Northwest) have now bred over one hundred American and Canadian Champions. It all started with Am. Can. Mexican and Bermudan and Columbian Ch. Beckwith's Copper Corn was a Group winner in five countries. He was

Ch. Wochica's Okeechobee Jake: Multiple Best in Show winner.

J. Luria.

breeder/owner/handled to all his wins. He sired fifteen Champions, and was the foundation sire for the Beckwith kennel. The foundation dam was Am. Can. Ch. Beckwith's Frolic of Yeo CDX, an import from the UK, and dam of twelve American Champions. Many dogs of their breeding have been nominated to the Hall of Fame.

CAROLEE
This influential kennel is owned by Shirley M. Goodman of Ontario. Her Ch. Goldendale Belle CD is the dam of five Champions, and is a combination of American and British bloodlines. The result of breeding on to Canadian and American dogs, has been many top winners, including one of the few Dual Champions, AFC Carolee's Something Special II CDX, WCX. He went on to sire Champions, and he died in 1990.

CLOVERDALE
Owned by Richard and Jane Zimmerman, Connecticut (North East), this kennel was founded in 1971 and it has developed into an important kennel. Ch. Cloverdale's Ringold Tobey is one of their many members of the Golden Retriever Club of America's Show Dog Hall of Fame. Another great bitch was Ch. Cloverdale Twin-Beau-D-Joy, owned by the Dalliares.

FEATHERQUEST
Rachel Page Elliott has long been one of America's most respected authorities on dog gait. Her unique, illustrated lectures on the subject have been hailed by audiences throughout the United States (including Hawaii and Alaska), Canada, Mexico, England, Scotland, Wales and the Scandinavian countries, Europe and Australia – and have done much to awaken breeders to the importance of recognizing the rights and wrongs in the way dogs move. When *Dogsteps* (largely

based upon the lectures) was published in 1973, the Dog Writers Association of America acclaimed it "Best Dog Book of the Year", and it continues to be the eminent book on dog gait.

'Pagey' Elliott was born in Lexington, Massachusetts, the youngest of a large family, who shared their lives with horses, dogs and other animals. She is a graduate of Radcliffe College. With her husband Mark, a retired orthodontist, she lives on a 60-acre farm along the Concord River in Carlisle (Mass), where they raised three children and have enjoyed an active participation in outdoor sports. Over the years the Elliotts have owned many breeds, but the main attention has been on Golden Retrievers. Foundation of their Featherquest kennel was Goldwood Toby, trained and handled by 'Pagey', and the first Golden to earn a Utility degree in Obedience. Toby's son, Tennessee's Jack Daniels, also owner-handled, was the first New England retriever to win a qualifying stake in licensed retriever trials. The Featherquest honour roll also includes many Show Champions.

GAYHAVEN
Owned by Sam and Betty Gay, their first home-bred Champion was Ch. Gayhaven Harmony CDX (co-owned with Marcia Schlehr), and she proved to be an outstanding dam. They have gone on to produce many Champions and sires and dams of Champions.

GOLDEN PINE
Started in the 1950s by Marilu Semans, this kennel has bred many influential Golden Retrievers of a good type. In the 1970s Nancy Kelly of Besaas, California carried on the Golden Pine prefix. Top dogs included Am. Can. Ch. Golden Pine Courvoisier CDX WC. Can. Ch. Golden Pine Gibson Solo became an outstanding sire in Canada. This kennel has bred over one hundred Champions since the 1950s.

GOLDRANGE
The Canadian-based Goldrange kennel is well-known for its influential stud dogs, starting with Ch. Goldrange Fine Fella of Yeo, and his son, Ch. Currahall's Karo of Goldrange. They have both made an indelible mark on the breed.

GOLD RUSH
Ann Johnson, New Jersey (East) purchased a family pet who became a top-winning Golden Retriever. This was Am. Can. and Bermudian Ch. Cummings Gold Rush Charlie, sire of Ch. Gold Rush's Great Teddy Bear, a tremendous winner in his own right. Their stud dogs have had a great effect on the breed.

KYRIE
Owned by Marcia Schlehr, Clinton, Michigan, this kennel was founded in the late 1950s. It has always been a small kennel with a limited breeding programme and restricted showing. Marcia's foundation bitch, Ch. Gayhaven Harmony CDX, produced Champions by four different sires. Two outstanding Kyrie dogs are Am. Can. Ch Gayhaven Lidiel (Am. Can. CDX, Am. WC) sire of eight American Champions and sixteen Canadian Champions, and his son, Am. Can. Ch. Kyrie Daemon (Am. CDX, WC, Can. CD), owned by Pat and Joan Nazark, who is also an outstanding sire.

LAURELL
Owned by Laura King of Ohio, the foundation for this kennel was Ch. Rusticana's Princess Teena

CD. Many typical Champions have been produced, notably by Ch. Laurell's Kilimanjaro, whose Champion offspring go into double figures.

MEADOWPOND
Owned by Cherie Berger, Michigan (North Central), founded in 1968, this all-purpose kennel has had many breed and Obedience title-holders, including Hall of Fame and GRCA outstanding dams. This kennel has imported from the Camrose, Noravon and Lislone kennels in the UK. One of the top Obedience dogs is Barrie Brown's OTCh Meadowpond Dust Commander.

PEPPERHILL
Owned by Jeffrey Pepper of New York, this kennel has produced many famous Champions including Ch. Cummings Dame Pepperhill, an outstanding producer whose daughters also made their mark as excellent producers. Ch. Pepperhill East Point Airily is in the Show Dog Hall of Fame. Ch. Russo's Pepperhill Poppy has proved to be an outstanding dam, and Am. Can. Ch. Pepperhill's Basically Bear is an influential sire.

SUNDANCE
Owned by Bill and Shirley Worley and Lisa Schultz, this kennel was started in the late 1950s. There are over one hundred Champions with the Sundance prefix, and many Hall of Fame members.

Other leading kennels include:
ANJAMAR owned by D. and M. McKenzie, Canada
BIRNAM WOOD, owned by Sylvia Donahey-Feeney, California (formerly Michigan and Wisconsin)
COLABAUGH owned by Janine Fiorito, New York (North East)
DAYSTAR owned by Randell and Zelia Bohsen, Missouri (Central)
FAERA owned by Rhonda Hovan, Ohio (Mid West)
GINGE owned by Ginger Gotcher, Texas (South Central)
GOLWING owned by Leslie Dove, Virginia (East)
KAZAK owned by Bernadette and David Cox, Washington (North East)
KRISHNA owned by Gloria Kerr, Arizona (South West)
MALAGOLD owned by Connie Gerstner, Wisconsin (North Central); NAUTILUS owned by Julie MacKinnon, Massachusetts (North East)
MEL-BACH owned by G. Mehlenbacher of Canada
ORIANA owned by B. and A. Mills of Canada
PEBWIN owned by Berna Hart Welch, Massachusetts (North East)
PEKAY owned by Pat Klausman, Georgia (South East)
RUSH HILL owned by Tonya Struble, Washington (North East)
SHADYWELL owned by C. MacDonald of Canada
SIGNATURE owned by Robin and John Stirrat, Missouri (Central)
SKYLER owned by J. and B. Taylor of Canada
STONEHILL FARM owned by Judy and Ray Laureand, New Jersey
SUNFIRE owned by R. Book and B. Biewer
SUNSHINE owned by Debra Berry, California (West)
SUNSHINEHILL owned by Elaine Fraze, Pennsylvania (East)

NAFC FCH Topbrass Cotton: The high-point Golden of all time at Field Trials.

TOPBRASS owned by Jackie Mertens and Judy Slayton, Illinois (Central), a kennel that has done well in all areas.
TWIN-BEAU-D owned by Nancy Dallaire, Massachusetts (East)
VANREEL owned by Gretchen Vandenberg and Denise Reel, Washington (North west)
BELVEDERE owned by Mercedes Hitchcock.

THE VERSATILE RETRIEVER

The above are primarily show kennels, although Meadowpond has produced a large number of Obedience title holders, and Topbrass is a major producer of Field and Obedience dogs. Sunfire is also known for Field and Obedience performers.

The trend in the USA in the last few years has been even more towards the 'specialist' dog. The majority of the best-known kennels concentrate on the show ring aspect, and there is a high level of competition for wins, especially for Group ('Variety' Group) and Best in Show wins, and for producing the highest number of Champions. Field Trial devotees also specialize in dogs for trial work; those dogs who do not make it to the Field Trial winning level (and it is an extremely demanding area of competition) often participate with distinction in Hunting Tests and as gundogs.

There are Golden fanciers who still believe in, and achieve, the capabilities of the truly versatile Golden. Not all compete for titles, but there are still Champions that hunt and serve as working gundogs; there are good-looking working dogs that may not complete a show title; and there are a few whose owners have the will and the resources to get a full range of titles. A few of these dogs of recent years deserve mention:

1. CH. BEAULIEU'S ACACIA O'DARNLEY, UDTX, JH, WCX (Jeanette Von Barby). Also a top-producing dam.
2. CH. ELYSIAN SKY HI DUBL EXPOSURE, TD, CDX, MH, WCX (Sandra Whicker). The first Ch. to place in Specialty Field Trial in many years).
3. CH. ELYSIAN'S LI'L LEICA REPRINT, UDT, JH, WC (Jeanette Von Barby). Best in Show Winner.
4. CH XIV KARAT SIMON SAYS SHOW UDT, SH (Gloria Marr). One of a litter of six who share numerous Show, Obedience, and Working titles.
5. CH BECKWITH'S MAIN EVENT, UDT, JH, WCX (Caroline McCormick).
6. CH BECKWITH'S EASTER CELEBRITY UDT, JH, WC (Christine Robertson MD).
7. CH. MEADOWPOND SIMON SEZ, UDT, JH, WC (Judy Super-Borton).
8. CAN. CH. COMSTOCK'S CARAMEL NUT, UDTX, SH. WCX, CAN. UD, WCX (Kathy Eddy). Also known for his daughter.
9. CH. COMSTOCK SUNFIRE O'HILLCREST, UDT, SH WCX (Kathy Eddy,VMD, B. Biewer, B. Book).
10. CH. WHIPALY'S COLABAUGH SENNA, UD, SH, WCX (Janine Fiorito).
11. AM.CAN.CH. HERON ACRES SANDCASTLE, MH, AM. CAN. UDTX, WCX (Elizabeth Drobac).

While the above is not a complete list of outstandingly titled Golden Retrievers, dedicated owner/trainers such as the above are essential in demonstrating that the breed retains its multiple capabilities as a truly versatile breed. The GRCA's has recently established the awards of VC (Versatility Certificate) and VCX (Versatility Certificate Excellent) to formally recognise Goldens with accomplishments in bench show, obedience, and field areas.

THE FIELD

By Nona Kilgore Bauer

RETRIEVER FIELD TRIALS

Retriever Field Trials in the USA are conducted under rules and procedures set down by the American Kennel Club. Licensed trials, where Championship points may be awarded, are sponsored by AKC licensed or member clubs, and only pure-bred retrievers over six months of age may be entered. The mechanics and requirements of each trial are determined by the Judges and the Field Trial Committee.

The dogs are run individually and are expected to retrieve any type of game bird under any and all conditions. They must walk at heel, sit quietly in the blind or on the line, and seek and retrieve the bird(s) when ordered to do so. They should retrieve quickly and briskly, without disturbing too much ground, and should deliver tenderly to hand. The AKC rules and standard procedure specifically state: "accurate marking is of primary importance. A dog which marks the fall of a bird, uses the wind, follows a strong cripple, and will take direction from his handler is of great value."

The regular stakes at a licensed Retriever Trial consist of two minor stakes, the Derby and the Qualifying, and two categories of major stakes where Championship points may be awarded; Amateur All-Age (including Owner-Handler Amateur All-Age) and Open All-Age (including Limited All-Age, and Special All-Age). Two individuals judge each stake, with their combined judging qualifications determined by AKC Regulations. All licensed trials must test the competing dogs both on land and in the water.

THE DERBY STAKE: This is open to dogs who have not reached their second birthday on the first day of the trial in which they are entered. A Derby Stake usually consists of three to four series of marking tests that include both land and water work. A Derby dog is not expected to handle or to perform blind retrieves. Tests are most commonly double retrieves, with an increased degree of difficulty (e.g. distance, terrain, hazards, etc.) in each successive series. As in every Stake, only dogs with satisfactory scores are called back to be tested in the next series.

THE QUALIFYING STAKE: This is open to dogs who have never won first, second, third or fourth place or a Judge's Award of Merit (JAM) in an Open All-Age, Limited All-Age or Special All-Age, an Amateur All-Age or Owner-Handler Amateur All-Age Stake, and to dogs who have not yet won two first places in Qualifying Stakes. A dog who is no longer eligible to run the Qualifying because he has placed or JAMed as stated, is said to be an "All-Age" or "Qualified" retriever.

Dogs entered in a Qualifying Stake are tested in four series consisting of a double or triple marked retrieve on land, a single or double land blind, followed by a water blind and a triple water marking test. The dog is required to honor the working dog in one series of marks. The degree of difficulty in each series is determined by the individual judge's standards, and in certain Qualifying Stakes, one may even find an occasional retired gun, poison bird or diversion shot.

OPEN ALL-AGE STAKE: Both professionals and amateurs compete. An Open All-Age entry may sometimes be limited to dogs who have previously earned a placement or JAM in an Open All-Age, Amateur All-Age or Owner-Handler All-Age Stake, the stake then being called a limited

All-Age Stake. An Open All-Age may also run a Special All-Age by limiting entry to dogs who have earned Qualified status during the previous calendar year.

AMATEUR ALL-AGE STAKE: Run for dogs with amateur handlers only, professional handlers being ineligible for competition. An Amateur All-Age may further limit its entry by holding an Owner-Handler All-Age Stake, which dictates that all dogs entered must be handled by an amateur who is also the registered owner of the dog.

AMATEUR ALL-AGE STAKE OPEN ALL-AGE STAKE: This is run in the same land/water sequence as the Qualifying Stake, but with a much greater degree of difficulty in each series. Marking tests might include quadruple retrieves, one or two retired guns, a very narrow corridor between the marks, with the distance of some retrieves exceeding 300 yards. Blinds are often multiple, longer (300 to 350 yards in typical) and more difficult. All-Age Stakes also incorporate greater complexity of terrain, land and water hazards and wind conditions into every test, further challenging those competitors seeking championship points. The dog is required to honor the working retriever in one of the series.

   During the past two decades, the degree of difficulty in Retriever Field Trials has challenged both dog and trainer to levels of excellence once considered impossible in retriever training. As the dogs and handlers have met and continue to meet or exceed those challenges, tougher and more creative conditions always seem to arise to test the retriever's ability and skill. These standards have not diminished the field trialer's enthusiasm for the sport. In many areas of the United States, entries in All-Age Stakes often exceed 100 dogs.

FIELD TRAINING YOUNG RETRIEVERS

By Mercedes Hitchcock

My field work started in October 1977, when I received a high-energy pup from Michigan. At seven weeks of age, he had one big priority in life: to retrieve! Through the years we have pursued that goal... from Long Island (NY) to Coto de Caza (CA), from Lake Charles (LA) to Edmonton (CAN). We recognize field trials as a challenging outdoor sport, and the training of the retriever as an intellectual exercise.

   The following program has been used over the years to work with puppies that will go into trial or hunting homes. Where the timetable is general, adapt it to the individual dog and his maturity level.

SEVEN WEEKS TO THREE MONTHS

Concentrate on crate and house training, allowing the puppy to remain with you in the same room to prevent problems. Use a leash on the pup as an 'umbilical cording' to guide or correct. Take walks with the pup for exploration and to build self-confidence. Make use of the pup's instinct to follow now, walk through high cover, ditches, wade, cultivate alertness and attentiveness on informal recalls. Teach your pup not to range too far from you; use a long line, but let it drag unless needed. Pup should be socialized with many people and other unfamiliar dogs once he has received his vaccinations. A pond with a gradual grassy slope is best for encouraging pup to get in the water. An older dog can entice the pup to jump in and swim. Above all, do not force; make it fun.

HR Ch. Holway Vodka: Owned by Mercedes Hitchcock and Terry Giffen Woods.

Every morning, after the pup has relieved himself, throw three to ten happy puppy bumpers (canvas work well). The pup must see your hand extended to throw. Give short throws at first, increasing distance till the pup runs out as far as you can throw. Always encourage the dog to return to you. Try for hand delivery, a sit is unimportant here. Run backward, arms open wide, using enthusiastic approval: "Good dog" "OK" – praising sincerely several times in each session. If the dog has natural desire (what you are looking for) he needs time to concentrate on his work. Constant babble can get in the way. If he runs to the dummy but will not pick up, you can kick it and repeat "fetch" happily. Quit if that does not work. It could be the day or the dog. If the pup has a low level of drive, try to limit the retrieves to three, but try to get all three. With this pup, do it early when the day is cool and he feels eager to move out. Any swimming the pup may do now is a benefit: coming in with you wading and short retrieves in the edge of the pond or pool are good.

THREE MONTHS TO SIX MONTHS

In general, sharpen control and basic Obedience. Take a good puppy class. This will prevent bad habits from becoming ingrained, and provide a foundation of positive control. You cannot control a dog in the field at 100 yards unless you can do so when he is at your side. In my puppy classes, we work on the problems, but also try to emphasize the fun retrieves and games, stressing the importance of flat out running and exercise. We encourage owners to work on controlled walking and start on reliable recalls. We develop good eye contact and start sit-stays gradually.

For land work, we use mostly very low cover and white bumpers or dead light pigeons occasionally if the pup has no mouth problem. It helps the dog learn to use his eyes when entering the area of the fall (too often pups will rely on their nose only). In focusing on the target as he runs out, the dog will learn to hold a straight line to the fall. School yards, golf courses, and parks can be utilized for stretching out marks; but try not to extend too far too fast. This can cause inaccuracy in hunting the area by working too short or wildly running past. Dummies can be thrown at distances under 80 yards, helping pup to go straight out and find the mark at this age.

If necessary, you can "salt" the area by putting several bumpers in the proximity of the fall before the throw so he is sure to find one as he runs through the area. Another crutch used with a young dog to extend marks and add drive: have the bird thrower toss a second bumper as the pup is running out (about halfway there). Your helper needs to yell or shoot a training pistol so the dog will see him. Use lots of angle back throws to accustom the dog to going past the bird thrower. Use canvas dummies while teething, after that use 2 and 3 inch rubber knobbies or canvas dummies. When the pup drops a dummy, he may be hot or tired. Watch the attitude and tail to determine when to end the session. Too little can be better than too much at this stage.

The single most effective marking drill I use with pups of this age is "contour" marks, to teach increased distance and going straight. The bird thrower stands in one place with several dummies and throws the mark. The pup runs a short distance for the retrieve, then the handler moves to the second of three predetermined lines to receive the dog. The handler sends him again, this time the distance increases and usually an obstacle has to be crossed. The handler moves to the third position to receive the pup. The dog sees the mark once more from the line with more distance and obstacles, e.g. cover, ditches, road, to drive through to the fall. This lets you see memory develop in the young dog and it builds confidence. The object of marking any young pup is to teach him to *succeed.* If the dog will not come straight in from the retrieve, the handler must use a long line; yard Obedience should also emphasize the recall.

Water work at this level should incorporate short swims and short retrieves in the pond or pool, increasing the distance in gradual increments. The retrieves are thrown straight in front of the pup (no angle entries) with the pup at the edge of the water at first. Gradually, the pup can be backed up from the shoreline. The handler should work on receiving the dummy before the dog shakes – something Goldens like to do upon emerging from a swim. Expect the pup to deliver to hand and then allow him to shake off the water. If the pup shows genuine drive now, let him retrieve over small islands, incorporating the land, water, land concept. The dummy can be thrown into cover at the edge of the water, but it should float in the water to prevent the dog from getting out on the far bank and running around (cheating) at this age. If the pup is reluctant to enter the water, a clip wing pigeon may be helpful as a mark.

SIX MONTHS TO NINE MONTHS

In general by this time, the pup should be crate-trained, house-trained, ride comfortably in a car, and exhibit friendliness with good social manners. The land work will consist mostly of single marks, increasing distance as the pup goes straight to the area. Most of the time, the dog should learn to find the dummy on his own, to develop perseverance, but if out of the area, the bird thrower can yell "hey, hey" to get the pup's attention to return to the area.

Easy doubles can be introduced, running the pup on a single, and then repeating this mark as the memory bird with a short retrieve to one side. Gradually, the distance of the second fall can be increased, as well as the difficulty of the memory bird.

One of the most important concepts that we have to teach in our trial training is not returning to an "old" fall, that is: the first one that the dog has retrieved. Derby tests can be challenging: when the dog smells the first bird crate as he runs out toward the second mark, or he sees the bird thrower from a different perspective and turns to go back. This consumes months of time in training a prospective trial dog; the dog of 18 to 20 months will usually begin to work predictably

Midas Belvedere Houston WCX: Owned by Mercedes Hitchcock.

*Midas
Belvedere
Houston in
action.*

Gary Hodges.

in training on this. Water work now adds increased distances and difficulty to the retrieves. Angle entries should be avoided during this period until the handler can correct the dog effectively for cheating.

During this period, most American trainers put the pup through the big step, the "Force Training", usually at six to eight months when the pup has all of the permanent teeth. Briefly, this incorporates forcing the dog to open his mouth while pinching the ear as the handler commands "fetch", in gradual stages until the dummy is on the ground. The "drop" is a part of the training to end mouth problems. The "hold"is taught as a separate exercise. With each step, the dog receives more pressure and this builds tolerance in the pup. After the handler completes the Force Training, the dog will usually be collar conditioned to the electronic collar. Initially the exercises of "sit" and "here" or "come", then the "sit to the whistle", basic to handling are reinforced with the collar. Steadiness can be strengthened now if need be. Bear in mind that you never teach a dog with the electric collar – it is a powerful reinforcement tool to be used with patience and expertise.

The sequence of advanced work starts with the handler sending the dog to a pile of dummies 20 to 30 feet away and then gradually increasing the distance. Next come the directed simple casts in the "baseball" drill: "overs" and "back". Finally the Double T drill extends this concept and the dog must stop to the whistle before running in a given direction.The water drills follow in sequence the above land work. The handler forces the dog to a pile across the narrow channel, usually 30 to 40 yards. After the dog understands that he must swim out and retrieve when given the command, the handler introduces water baseball casts. Finally, the trainer teaches the shore breaking program, where the dog must stay in the water, using channel swims and swim-bys. This training is very important for an American trial dog; our trials are won or lost on the water!

The most complex drill used by most trial trainers is called the Wagon Wheel, invented by professional retriever trainer, Rex Carr. The drill teaches the dog the fine lines of distinction between lining and casting direction. The entire program, as outlined, can take from a year to a year and a half of actual training time. During this period marks should be continued to keep the dog's interest high.

In a teaching situation, dogs are as individual as children. There is no one way to develop the talent, or a hard and fast timetable. You cannot make the training too simple. The trainer must *teach* the dog, over and over again. To build the pup's confidence he should experience three consecutive successes in any training session. Confidence is the foundation upon which future success is built.

EXPERT ADVICE
The following is advice from Ron Wood of the Dog Wood Kennel.

"I have been asked to do the impossible, briefly describe techniques needed to train a young retriever. This is a topic I clearly love but daily find how little I know. Here are a few of my ideas (not legally mine, but ideas shared by many other trainers) on how to obtain the very best retriever possible.

"Breeding is of utmost importance, so the very best sire and dam should be picked. Pay particular attention to appearance, temperament, field abilities (shooting dog or field trial). Having decided on the best possible breeding, you are ready to pick your pup. I like good eye contact, eagerness, desire for human contact etc. At seven weeks unofficial training begins. This may very well be the most important and most overlooked part of a young dog's training. During the first few months your pup develops an attitude that will stay with him his entire life. This is your time to mold the very best retriever possible (a wild uncontrollable maniac or a well mannered pup able to distinguish right from wrong).

"I prefer to start basic training somewhere between six to twelve months, depending on the pup's maturity. At this time a more disciplined obedience program is needed, followed by force fetch (one of the most important parts needed in reaching the final product). After the force fetch is completed, plenty of bird marks (land and water) are in order. It is at this time that the dog's abilities and maturity level should be evaluated. The options are to continue to elevate his marking and hunting skills or to start him handling (sitting on the whistle and taking hand signals). If your young dog has the ability, I firmly believe he should be advanced to handling skills accompanied by lots of bird marks."

Chapter Fourteen

GOLDEN RETRIEVERS WORLDWIDE

Britain is the Golden Retriever's country of origin, and therefore breeders in other countries have imported dogs from the breed's homeland when first establishing new kennels and new lines. This trend has continued, and so British influence is apparent worldwide. It is a pity that some of the leading North American lines have not been exported. To date their influence is largely restricted to the United States and Canada.

SCANDINAVIA

The Golden Retrievers are of a high standard in Scandinavia, and this I know from first-hand knowledge, for over the years I have judged many times in Sweden, Norway, Denmark and Finland. I have judged a rare triple – the Stockholm International Show, the Oslo International Shows, known as the Crufts of their countries, and Golden Retriever bitches at Crufts itself.

SWEDEN

EARLY HISTORY
The first Golden import we know of was from Mrs Charlsworth's Noranby kennel, Noranby Juno, who came in 1927. Juno had a litter when mated to the imported Kim of Kentford, but these events were not as important as the import in 1950 of Barthill Fanny, in whelp to Strelley Starlight, who was sire of the British dual CC winner, Wyckwold Desperado, and grandsire of the lovely Ch. Flax of Wham. The resulting litter of six puppies laid the foundation of the breed in Sweden, especially through the Borghalla kennel. At this time the beginning of the influential Stubblesdown imports came to the Hedetorpet kennel, and they campaigned Ch. Stubblesdown Tinker.

Then, what was to become one of Sweden's greatest kennels came into being – the Apport kennel, whose foundation bitch came from Borghalla. Apport also owned, at this time, a well-known stud dog, Count Leo of Little Compton (Duke of Timothy – Honeyat Derry Down Dilly). The Apport's first litter in 1955 made breed history, containing Dual Ch. Apports Ambassadeur, FT Ch. Apports Ascot, and two Champions, Ali and Annette. Apports brought Stubblesdown Begay to Sweden in whelp to FT Ch. Stubblesdown Larry, and again two puppies, born 1958, proved very influential – Ch. Apports Larry Jr. and Apports Joy.

In 1960 the Hedetorpet kennel brought in Int. & Nordic Ch. Azor vd Kruidberg (Martin of Aldercarr – Castelnau Roundelay). This dog had English bloodlines, although he was imported from the Netherlands. Later Int.S.Nu.Ch. Whamstead Jess (Boltby Sonja – Whamstead Jerinthia of

*Int. Ch.
Dewmist
Chrysander: A
top stud dog
for the
Dewmist
kennel.*

*Henric
Fryckstrand.*

Jeanara) was mated to Azor: she produced the great winner of that era, Int. Ch. Hedetorpets Honey, born 1963.

Another kennel of great influence was Sandemar, founded on Int.Ch. Sandemars Azurra (Ch. Apports Larry Jr. – Bonnie Av Sickelsjo). Sandemar imported two more Stubblesdowns, Int. Ch. Shaun and Angus, and that continued the type of the earlier imports. Sandemar then imported Int. Ch. Glenessa Waterbird of Stenbury who tended to change the type. Among the many winners he sired was the first bitch to gain the title of Int. & Scan.Ch. – Sandemars W. Grandezza (Int. Nord.U.Ch. Glennessa Waterbird of Stenbury – Whamstead Queen). A stud dog, again of a different type, was brought in from Denmark. This was Ch. Wessex Timmy Tinker (Dk.U.Ch. Anbria Tarlatan – Dk.U.Ch. Anbria Joriemour Lisbeth), and he sired many winners and Champions, including Int. Ch. Apports Country Boy, and a daughter, Int.Ch. Daisy, who was one of the top dogs all breeds in 1969.

INFLUENTIAL IMPORTS

The Hedetorpet kennel imported and made up Ch. Stolford Sea Bird and Stolford Larkspur. Larkspur was a great brood and produced Int.Ch. & FT Ch. Hedetorpets Bijou, the first bitch to obtain both titles. In 1969 Hedetorpet brought in Int.Ch. & FT Ch. Coxy (Int. Dk.SU.Ch. Byxfield Cedar – Pakche), a top winner 1972 and 1973 and sire of many winners and workers.

Sandemar brought in from the UK and made up Ch. Cabus Clipper, a younger brother to Ch. Camrose Cabus Christopher. They also imported from the UK the top winners and title gainers in Sweden, Ch. Glennessa Helmsman – who went BIS at the Stockholm International – and Ch. Synspur Iona. Sandemar later imported two dogs who became famous as winners and sires in Scandinavia, Ch. Caliph of Yeo (Ch. Stolford Happy Lad – Ch. Deerflite Endeavour of Yeo), and the personality-plus dog who gained his UK Sh.Ch. title and then went to Sweden to become Sh.Ch. & Nor.Ch. Glenavis Barman (Ch. Camrose Cabus Christopher – Irish Ch. Mandingo Marigold).

ABOVE: A line-up of Dewmist Champions (left to right): D. Shardonnay, D. Sonatina (3CCs), Ch. D. Santinella, Ch. D. Syretta and Ch. D. Solitaire. *Henric Fryckstrand.*

BELOW: Ch. Guldklimpens Olga The Comtesse (left), and Ch. Gyrima Zacharias (right) with six daughters – four with CCs as juniors. *Tina Lindeman.*

Ch. Dewmist Solitaire, a member of an outstanding litter.   *Henric Frykstrand*

The Dainty kennel has been a force to be reckoned with in Sweden for many years. One of their first influential stud dogs was Davern Fergus, a brother of UK Ch. Davern Figaro, who came to Sweden in 1971. Other imports for this famous kennel included: Ch. Alseras Capello (Ch. Camrose Cabus Christopher – Lindys Matilda of Alsera), runner-up for All Breeds Dog of the Year in 1981, and the famous brother and sister, Ch. Stenbury Sealord and Ch. Stenbury Seamusic. There have been many lovely winning Daintys, and among so many I must mention the top brood, Dainty's Pretty Face, and the important stud dog and winner, Dainty's Having It All. The Dainty kennel has also used AI from the UK and from Denmark, and offspring by Sh.Ch. Nortonwood Silvanus, Dainty's Son of Sky and Stormwarning have CACIBs, as do Dainty's Brittania Rules and Blues In The Night. The Pallywood kennel won well with Int.Ch. Pengelli Lysander.

In 1974 a new era began with the Knegaren's kennel UK importation of Ch. Deremar Donald and his two sisters, Ch. Denise and Deborah. They were by Ch. Davern Figaro out of Ch. Deremar Rosemary, who was one of the few genuine dual-purpose Goldens of her era in the UK. Donald was a very influential stud dog in the show ring and in the field. His get included Ch. & FT Ch. Teachers Melvyn, Int. Ch. Kimbalee Colonel Peron, the lovely Ch. Dancing Elinda (I remember making this bitch BOB at Skokloster), her brother, Ch. Earl Dinwiddy, and for Knegarens itself, Int.Ch. Knegarens Heidi.

There have been many Knegarens winners, as well top studs such as Int.Ch. Dewmist Chrysander. The Knegaren and Dewmist kennels imported Styal Samarkand, and the top winner producer for Knegaren and Dewmist has been Int. Ch. Sansue Golden Arrow. Dewmist has bred and owned many title-holders as well as those already mentioned from the UK. Ch. Gyrima Zacharias sired an outstanding litter for Dewmist which contained Nor. Champions Dewmist Shardonnay, Santinella, Syretta, Solitaire, and Sonatina with three CACs. Another 'star' in 1991 was Dewmist Deidre Dee.

The Ringmaster has made up many Champions since 1966, based on the Yeo bloodlines, they have also won at Field Trials. The Dream Max kennel has successfully combined their earlier top-producing lines with their imports from the UK, Nortonwood Secreto and NU.Ch. Nortonwood Travers.

Their winners have included Ch. Dream Max Never Say Never Again, and the young 'stars' for Dream Max include Dream Max Christmas Adventure. A kennel that has produced many winners is Guldklimpen; one of note was Ch. Guldklimpens Tarzan. Ch. Gulkdlimpens Olga The Comtesse has won top awards, and she has been a marvellous show and brood bitch for Festival's kennel. At one stage, seven of her daughters had taken 18 CACs – Nor. Ch. Festivals Prairie Primrose just one of note.

The working side of the breed has been well served. In the early seventies the Duvkullan kennel bought Duckflight Dik Dik, who became a FT Ch. and a good brood bitch producing a good working line. Duvkullan also imported Rambler of Maar, who made up into a FT Ch. Imports have come in from Holway, Ardyle and Standerwick to improve the working lines. Pickups and Respons are both working kennels who have had great success; Respons has campaigned many to become Dual Champions.

In a book of this kind I cannot cover all the Swedish kennels, and I apologise for any I have missed out. However, the following, along with those already mentioned, have played an important part in the development of the Golden Retrievers in Sweden: Combine, Crusade, Dasty, Delindas, Fairfax, Ferryside, Friendship's, Greensticks, Gullbackens, Kimbalee, Lucretias, Moorlac, Moviestar's, Pallywoods, Teachers, Twinkle, Solstrimman and Yellows. In 1990 there were over 3,000 registrations of Golden Retrievers.

NORWAY

In 1954 the first Goldens were registered at the Norwegian Kennel Club, imported from the UK. They were Pennard Golden Tosca, Mellowgold Jester, Prinmere Alistair and Somerscot Timothy. Tosca had one litter to Jester but nothing else really happened until 1959 when the bitches Redstead Belinda (Arbrook Alresford Eclipse – Ecstasy of Arbrook) and Seaspel of Boyers (Pennard Golden Rally – Seaspray of Boyers) were imported. In 1962 they were mated to a Danish dog visiting Norway, Int.Ch. Philips Tais Flapore.

The first Golden Retriever to be made up in Norway, in 1964, came from the UK. This was Ch. Drexholme Chrysler Venture (Ch. Drexholme Herb Robert – Boltby Sedate of Drexholme). The next year saw the first bitch made up, Ch. Camrose Una (Ch. Camrose Tallyrand of Anbria – Camrose Quentanya). Another well-known import of that era was Boltby Brigand. The Tais kennel in Denmark sent Tais Farah, Jasmine and Nicholas. In 1966 came the first Hedetorpets from Sweden, Ch. Hedetorpets Guy, who was also the first Golden to be BIS at a Kennel Club Show, plus Marigold, Moonraker and Morning Star.

Two important studs to come from the UK during the 1960s were Brambledown Harvester, a son of Ch. Camrose Nicolas of Westley, and Cabus Clarion, sired by Ch. Camrose Tallyrand of Anbria. Two top-quality bitches came from the Camrose kennels and founded two important kennels. They were NU.Ch. Camrose Tudina (Ch. Camrose Tallyrand of Anbria – Kirsty of Altarnun) for the Gitle kennel, and Camrose Evensky (Ch. Camrose Cabus Christopher – Camrose Kertrude) for the

Nordic Ch. Mjaerumhogdas Crusader: This dog stood at stud in the UK for a short time, and also won a CC.
David Dalton.

Kargul kennel. In the seventies some more important stud dogs were imported from the UK: NU.Ch. Camrose Voravey (Camrose Octavius – Camrose Westley Loretta) for the Mjaerumhogda kennel; NU.Ch. Davern Lion Lotcheck (Ch. Davern Figaro – Davern Gabriella) for the Boana kennel; Int. Scan. Ch. Sansue Sunlover, the first Golden with this title; NU.Ch. Styal Scimiter for the Astown kennel; and NU.Ch. Likely Lad of Yeo and NU.Ch. Noravon Lucius, who not only won well but also produced winners all over Scandinavia for the Mjaerumhogda kennel. One of his most famous sons was NU.Ch. N & S.L.Ch. Chribas Crackerjack, who I made BOB from Veteran at the Oslo International.

AI has been used with success over the years. In 1974 Ch. Camrose Cabus Christopher produced ten puppies to a Norwegian bitch. One of the best from the litter, NU.Ch. Spervikbuktens Philip, was one of the top dogs All Breeds for some years. Since the beginning of the eighties the top-producing kennel is Mjaerumhogda, now in double figures for Champions. They have sent winning influential Goldens all over Scandinavia, and one of these big winners, NU.Ch. Mjaerumhogda Crusader, came to the UK for a short time and sired winners – Crusader himself won a Challenge Certificate.

Using AI, Mjaerumhogda bred a litter sired by the long-dead Ch. Camrose Cabus Christopher. They kept Nuch Mjaerumhogda Top Hit who has had some excellent wins. Thor came to the UK's Camrose kennel, and, to date, has won one Challenge Certificate. Top Score is a Canadian.Ch. The Waterloo kennel has had great success with NU.Ch. Mjaerumhogda Limelight. Two further great Champions were owned by the Friendship kennel in Sweden, Mjaerumhogda Golden Look and Int. Ch. Classic Sound.

In 1991 Mjaerumhogda make up or bred six Champions. They were Nor. Champions Linchael Silver Spirit, Tasvane Time Bee, Jako's Mascot, Mjaerumhogda Glint O'Gold, Mjaerumhogda Top Hit, and Can. Ch. Mjaerumhogda Top Score. During 1990 the top-winning bitch in Norway was Nor. Ch. Floprym Home Made Hot Dog (Janward Dollar – Floprym American Dream), owned by the Floprym kennel. The ViVi kennel has done well with Nor. Ch. Sansue Lollipop ViVi. Flying the British flag is Ch. Shalnimore Baronet, a son of Sh.Ch. Nortonwood Silvanus out of a Dabess bitch.

Golden Retrievers have become more and more popular in Norway. In 1970 there were 243 registrations; in 1990 here were over 2,000 registrations.

FINLAND

The first two Goldens in Finland were registered in 1959, and they were imported for Field Trials. They were Holcot Sweep and Woodbarn Autumnglint. In 1960 Peter of Elvey became the first Finnish Champion. Autumnglint was mated to him and produced the first Finnish-bred litter in 1962. In the same year Rivertrees Larry (Ch. Simon of Westley – Rivertrees Melody Maid of Kersey) was imported from the UK, and he was quickly made up into a Champion. In 1965 two Goldens came from the Apport kennel in Sweden, and Ch. Apports Corinna founded the Woodhill kennel. Corinna's mating to the Swedish dog, Ch. Glennessa Waterbird of Stenbury, produced one of the top dogs of the time, Ch. Blond Boy of Woodhill.

In 1970 the Leavenworth kennel (well-known for its lovely Cocker Spaniels) imported Pride of the Morn of Petrina as its foundation bitch. This kennel also imported SF.U.Ch. Deerflite Summer Storm. In 1975 the Woodhill kennel imported Whitewater Patricia from Ireland. Her influence was great and still is today for she lies behind many of Finland's top dogs.

The Woodhill kennel continued to produce many winners, and in the 1980s AI was used from Camrose Fidelio of Davern, and the progeny have been incorporated into the Woodhill lines. The Reflect kennel imported Noravon Cornelius (a son of Ch. Nortonwood Faunus); he became a Champion and an influential sire. Reflect also owned and made up into Champions Deerflite Daffodil and Thenford Hamish, both from the UK. The Majik kennel had the good stud dog, Ch. Mjaerumhogda Your Choice, and also imported, from Britain, Dabess Wilberforce and Braydan

Int. Ch. Karvin Ultimatum, based in Finland.

Int. Ch. Karvin Corleone, one of the stars of the Karvin kennel.

Star Attraction. Their dog, Majik Johnny B.Goode, was-top winning Golden in Finland in 1989. The Karvin kennel imported and gained titles with two dogs from the UK, Linchael Ravel and Lovehayne Darter, and they have made their mark at stud.

In 1990 five dogs from the Karvin kennel gained their titles. They were: F.Ch. & FT.Ch. Karvin Quartz-Amor, SF.Ch.Karvin Corleone, SF.Ch. Karvin Uniform, SF.Ch. Karvin Union Bell and SF.OB.Ch. Karvin Toffie. Further Karvin imports were SF.Ch. Chevanne Snow N'Ice and Gunhill's Dalbury. In the 1970s about 120 Goldens were registered; in 1990 there were about 2,000 registrations.

DENMARK
The first Golden Retrievers that we know of in Denmark were imported in 1957. Vagabond of Coldharbour and Empshott Charming Lady produced the first litter in 1958, and these puppies were the foundation for the Tais kennel. One of the puppies become Int. Ch. Philips Tais Flapore, and he was well used at stud. The early sixties saw the importation of Taddington Lady Smock, Corn-Dolly, and Taddington Bellringer, who became a Champion. Camrose Quixote, a son of Int. Dual Ch. David of Westley was imported by the Attemosegaard kennel. He became a Champion, and although he died young, at five years old, he left his mark at stud. The Wessex kennel started their long line of winning dogs with the imports Anbria Laurel, Dk.U.Ch. Anbria Tarlatan, and Dk.U.Ch. Anbria Joriemour Lisbeth.

The mid-sixties saw two outstanding show and stud dogs imported from the UK – Int. & Dk.Ch. Honeyat The Viking to the Attemosegaard kennel, and Int.& Dk.Ch. Byxfield Cedar, Kennel Skidoo. They both had excellent show careers but they were completely different types, so never met! During the sixties many good imports came from the Camrose, Anbria, Westley kennels in the UK, followed by imports from Crouchers, Sansue and Lacons. The Lacons kennel sent a dog of great influence, born in 1976, to the Beechforest kennel. This was Int.Ch. Lacons Honey Lover (Ch. Sansue Tobias – Sh.Ch. Lacons Candy Floss).

Since 1968 the Tallygold kennel has been a force to reckon with; their stud dogs have carried on generation after generation. Those of note include Int. Ch. Crouchers Xavier (Ch. Stradcot Simon of Crouchers – Anbria Selina), and from Norway, with pure Camrose breeding, Nor. Ch. Camillo (Nor. Ch. Camrose Voravey – Cassata of Camrose). Successful offspring include Xavier's son, Matthew, a successful sire in his own right; Camillo's son, another winner producer, Tallygold Hot Chocolate, and the lovely bitch, Golden Joy's Polly Peachum (Matthew – Westley Dellajoy), a Group winner. Another big winner sent from the UK was Dk. Ch. Int. Ch. Lawnwoods Nimrod. The Reco kennel has won well with Linchael Star of Africa, and previously owned Nortonwood Telstar. FT champions have shown the influence of Holway imports.

Golden Retrievers are very popular in Denmark with registrations around 2,000.

THE REST OF EUROPE

Europe, excluding Scandinavia and the UK, is the next part of the Golden Retriever story. Europe is controlled, canine-wise, by the Federation Cynologique Internationale (FCI), with the exception of the UK which is run by the Kennel Club. The whole of Europe, except for Sweden, Norway and the UK, have no quarantine rules for dogs, so dogs can be shown over a tremendous area, and over the last ten years the breeding lines have become very inter-related throughout Europe.

I remember judging Golden Retrievers at the Bundessieger, the great German Show at Dortmund, in October 1985. I gave BOB to a dog from Denmark, and I was surprised that anybody should travel so far!

GERMANY

The first litter of Golden Retrievers registered in Germany was born on April 4th 1962. The dam was the English-bred Linnet of Essendene; the sire was a Dutch dog descended from Ch. Masterstroke of Yeo, namely Bull of John vd Harstenhock. The second litter in Germany was also born in 1962. This was sired by a dog imported from the UK out of a bitch from the USA. The dog was called Don, the bitch was Cragmounts Tessa. In the following years there were a few litters and only six puppies per litter were raised (German Kennel Club rule).

In 1963 a club was formed to take care of all the Retriever breeds, and right from the start they introduced very strict breeding regulations. Considering the breeding potential available at the time, this had a rather adverse effect on progress. Germany's geographical placement meant it was convenient for interested breeders to use stud dogs in other European countries. Breeding restrictions are still strict. All breeding stock has to be X-rayed for hip dysplasia, and eye tests must be carried out annually, or before mating. Selection tests, and a somewhat controversial temperament test, are compulsory. Since the beginning of 1990 all dogs are given a computer score based on the hip results of parents, siblings, offspring if any, etc. In 1990 a Golden Retriever Club was recognised by the German Kennel Club.

The Mill Lane kennel imported Camrose Mellomist (Ch. Davern Figaro – Camrose Fillipa Thisbe), born in 1976. She was made into a German Champion, and is behind so many Champions. I remember giving the Certificate to Ch. Guinevere of Mill Lane, one of her lovely daughters, who has bred on, producing more winners for Mill Lane. Ritzilyn Top Gun imported from the UK is siring winners and doing well himself.

Little Lizzie of Mill Lane.

David Dalton.

A group of the Mill Lane Golden Retrievers in Germany.

David Dalton.

Baltic Golden Melinda, bred and owned by Hilary Vogel in Germany.

World Champion Standfast Angus, based in the Netherlands.

The Redpine kennel has bred many winners including Int. Ch. Alice of Redpine (by Westland Sunshine), and Ch. Baika of Redpine (by Int. Ch. Lawnwoods Nimrod). The Baltic kennel have produced many winners including Int. Ch. Baltic Golden Gwendy, Baltic Golden Highness, and Ch. Baltic Golden Echo, out of Int. Ch. Master Melody born 1975. Golden Retriever registrations are around 700.

SWITZERLAND

The first litter of Golden Retrievers was registered in Switzerland in 1929. The sire was Diva, and the dam was Prim of Woolley (Bronze of Woolley – Balvaig). They had a second litter in 1933. Then there was a gap until 1949 when a dog Vestale de St. Jean du Bois (Pennard Golden Crispin – Tea de St. Jean de Bois) was imported from France. Her litter to Orix de St. Jean du Bois, in 1949, was registered under the kennel name of Reneveyres. In 1950 four dogs were imported from the UK; two from the Elsiville kennel, and in 1951 Stubbings Golden Dolphin joined this little group and interest began to grow. In 1987 The Retriever Club of Switzerland, an All Breed Retriever Club, came into being.

Early influential imports from the UK were: Swiss Ch. Thenford Maggie May (Deerflite Paragon – Thenford Part Piece) born 1973, Swiss Ch. Camrose Listrender (Ch. Cabus Janville Defenter – Camrose Wistansy) born 1970, the show dog and trained Mountain Rescue and Avalanche Rescue work dog, Swiss Ch. Rooftreetop Badi (Ch. Davern Figaro – Rooftreetop Betula) born 1976, Int. Ch. Catcombe Calibre (Catcombe Cupid – Amber Charm of Catcombe) born 1977, and his daughter, Int. Ch. Sevenhills Chesham (Int. Ch. Catcombe Calibre – Vimy Whinchat Piece) born 1979.

The Derrybeg kennel imported Int.Ch. Styal Samourai, Swiss Ch. Noravon Romulus, Swiss Ch. Styal Snow Storm, and many Derrybeg winners. The Westland kennel owned Int. Ch. Catcombe Calibre and bred Int. Ch. Westland Sunshine. The Chivas kennel campaigned Ch. Bimrigg Drummerboy, Ch. Chivas I Am Cardhu, and the Funnyline kennel has won well with Ch. Rossbourne King Chivas and Swiss Ch. Int. Ch. Amirene Intrepid. The Sevenhills kennel winners included Swiss Ch. & Int. Ch. Sevenhills Chesham, born 1979, plus many other Sevenhills winners and workers.

BELGIUM

There is very little information available on the Golden Retriever in Belgium in the early post-war period; those that are known about came chiefly from the UK for gundog work. In 1969 Holway Joker was imported and became an Int. Champion. His daughter, Int.Ch. Vitesse would certainly have been a Dual Champion, had there been such a title in those days.

The Glen Sheallag kennel has imported many famous winners, workers, and sires from the UK. They include Int. Ch. Lawnwoods Woodpecker of Nortonwood (Sh.Ch. Westley Munro of Nortonwood – Alfresco Spirit) born in 1982, and Int. Ch. and winner of three Field Trials, Ch. Bramhills Lochinvar (Sh. Ch. Stirchley Saxon – Bramhills Briar Rose). Among so many lovely bitches I must mention Ch. Orange Juice of Glen Sheallag (Ch. Jamescroft Squire – My Shadow of Glen Sheallag) who I made Best Bitch at the Belgian Retriever Club in 1992. The Du Val D'Alvaux kennel had the outstanding Int. Ch. Nortonwood Foregoer (Ch. Nortonwood Faunus – Nortonwood Serein) – I remember giving him one of his early wins. This kennel also campaigned Int. Ch. Nortonwood Thecia and Ch. Lawnwood Rumble Tumble from the UK, and they have brought in Swedish (Moviestar) lines.

The Lakeside Cottage and Wheatons kennels imported from the UK the winner, worker and good sire, Int. Ch. Styal Sungleam (Sh. Ch. Nortonwood Checkmate – Styal Solacea). The Roy Black Family kennel imported Westley Cumgen (Sh. Ch. Stirchley Saxon Westley Julianna) from the UK, and the Knippenborg's Ch. Jamescroft Squire (Sansue Castalian – Jamescroft Magic Miranda) was another British import. The Noroy Du Plessy kennel imported Ch. Mjaerumhogdas Goldman (Janward Dollar – Nor.Ch. Mjaerumhogdas Veronica) from Norway.

HOLLAND

The Golden Retriever made its first appearance in Holland in the thirties. The breed was imported from the UK mainly for work, and dogs came from the Heydown and Noranby kennels. They were rarely shown but their working abilities left a good impression. There was quite a gap due to the war, and then Mrs Van Schelle imported two British litter sisters, Pennard Golden Genista and Pennard Golden Garland. They were sired by Stubbings Golden Nicholas, a good sire in the UK, out of Pennard Golden Gem. Mrs. Van Schelle later imported Masterstroke of Yeo, who was an excellent worker, gained his title and was an influential sire. Also around this time Mrs Van Mourik imported from the UK Melody Abess, in whelp to Ch. Colin of Rosecott. Melody Abess later obtained her title.

No account of the early days would be complete without mentioning Mrs C. van Crevel, who owned the influential show and stud dog Ned. Ch. Bosco Brit (Capaul Neptune – Readyfaith Amber), and the Dutch-bred Dual Ch. Andy Van Sparrenrode. Mrs van Crevel and Baroness Snouckaert van Schauberg founded the Golden Retriever Club of the Netherlands in 1956. Today the Golden Retriever is the most popular breed in Holland. The GRCN has more than 7,000 members, and entries at the GRCN Championship Show in the past years exceeded 600. Other early British imports who gained their titles are Echo of Ulvin, Happy Lass of Ulvin, Chieftain of Ulvin, Weyland Curfew, Whamstead Gaye, Alresford Lovely Lady, Lindys Mary Rose and Lindys Lysander. Important dogs of the seventies: Int. Ch. Skidoos Brigitta (Int. Ch. Byxfield Cedar – Sansue Aleta), and Ch. Nelson Van De Adnorstee (Ch. Honeygolds Animato – Amber).

Moving on to the eighties and up to the present time, the Hellacious Acres kennel has imported from the UK and made up some lovely stock, including: Stirchley Seth (Ch. Nortonwood Faunus – Sansue Wanda of Stirchley), Ch. Noravon Amos (Ch. Westley Samuel – Noravon Melissa), Dutch Ch. Westley Beedee (Ch. Jescott Galahad – Ch. Westley Martha), and Ch. Westley Cathrina (Sh. Ch. Stirchley Saxon – Westley Julianna). There have been many title holders from this kennel, and judging in Germany in 1992, I gave BOB to Ch. Mack Labell Of The Hellacious Acres (Nor. Ch. Mjaerumhogdas Goldman – Ch. Westley Cathrina). He went on to win BIS and impressed me very much.

Dutch Ch. Westley Floyd, born 1982 (Sh. Ch. Lacons Enterprise – Ch. Westley Mabella), imported from the UK by Miss Klinkenberg, has been an important sire. The High Endeavour kennel imported the good winner and sire, Int. & Dutch Ch. Chevanne Mighty Endeavour (Ch. Styal Scott of Glengilde – Orchis Crystal Clear of Chevanne,) and also his brother. The v/h Wiekse Veld kennel imported from the UK and made up into a Dutch Champion, Aradias Apricot Whirl (Ch. Stolford Likely Lad – Bryanstown Serenade), and she proved a good brood bitch.

The vd Beerse Hoeve kennel has had some big winners. Dutch Ch. Mabella vd Beerse Hoeve is one of many, but at this time their greatest winner is the British import Twice World Champion, Dutch Ch. Standfast Angus (Nor. Ch. Mjaerumhogdas Crusader – Ch. Westley Ramona). I judged this outstanding dog when he went BIS at the Belgian Retriever Club Championship Show in 1992. There are many enthusiastic breeders in Holland, keen to improve the breed and they have imported dogs from well-known European kennels bringing in all the best known bloodlines. The result has been, over the years, a steady rise in the standard of the dogs seen in the show ring.

FRANCE
One of the first Goldens to carry the title French Champion was Noranby Jemima, born 1927 (FT.Ch. John of Auchencheyne – Ch. Noranby Jeptha). A picture in *Hutchinson's Dog Encyclopaedia* shows Golliwog of St. Cyran bred, owned and trained by Madame la Vicomtesse de Quenetain, sired by Anningsley Candidate out of French Ch. Noranby Jemima. The Kiplings kennel has imported from the UK, and then bred on some lovely Goldens including Int. Ch. Beamsley Brodie (Ch. Westley Topic of Sansue – Ch. Telmah Anabel of Beamsley), Int.Ch. Marymor Miles (Westley Joshua – Alveston Valmy), and I remember judging in Paris at the French Championship Show and giving the BOB to Int. Ch. Kiplings Burlington Bertie (Ch. Marymor Miles – Ch. Beamsley Brodie). Another big winner was Int. Ch. Kiplings Vienna Waltz (Ch. Marymor Miles – Ch. Beamsley Brodie).

The Glevum kennel had success with Ch. Lawnwoods Gideon (Sh.Ch. Westley Munro of Nortonwood – Gaiety Pink Sugar at Lawnwood), and Gyrima Etoile. The Ktema Eis Aei kennel imported from the UK Garbank Career Girl (Ch. Ninell Rambruen – Garbank Faberge). The Kissimee kennel brought in from from the UK a dog, who not only did top winning, but also Field Trial qualified. This was Int. Ch. Sherida Viceroy (Ch. Sherida Sirdar – Sherida Sayyida). The Du Pontias kennel had two Int. Ch. bitches, Afton Du Pontias and Butterfly Du Pontias (Ch. Bimrigg Drummerboy of Chivas – Chivas Ivy). The Gwin Ru kennel imported the British Ch. Rossbourne Pamela (Sh. Ch. Melfricka Kudos of Rossbourne – Rossbourne Truffle), and Rossbourne Virginia (Sh. Ch. Rossbourne Harvest Gold – Rossbourne Spring Love).

EIRE
Ireland, Golden Retriever-wise, is split as it is politically; the North is controlled by the English Kennel Club. The All Breeds Championship Show at Belfast is run under the English Kennel Club rules and the highest award is the English Kennel Club's Challenge Certificate. The South, the separate country Ireland, is ruled by the Irish Kennel Club under the umbrella of the FCI. Their top event is the St. Patrick's Day Show at Ballsbridge, and the highest award is the Irish Kennel Club's Green Stars.

The first two Golden Retrievers registered with the Irish Kennel Club might never have even come to Ireland, for there is no record of them ever having been entered at a show or Field Trial. They were Mrs Escombe's Cubbington Beauty (Thaxted Binks – Stagden Cross Gleam) born 1923, and Cubbington Drake (Triumph – Ottershaw Honey) born 1921. Mrs Charlsworth (Noranby) lived for a time in Ireland and must have had her dogs with her. In 1952 Mrs Joyce King (Leygore) moved to Cork and had her first bitch, Wyndolph Golden Charm (Sh. Ch. Trooper of Matsonhouse – Wyndolph Chereen) born 1948. Mrs King brought from England Earl of Stanton (Stubbings Golden Zephyr – Elizabeth of Monterey) who was mated to Charm, and they were the sire and dam of Ir.Ch. Leygore Calcharm. Leygore was the foundation of other kennels such as Seamourne, Tyrol, Lissamore.

The kennel that brought the Golden Retriever to the fore as a show dog and as a worker was the Twists' Bryanstown kennels. When they lived in Ireland, Cynthia Twist imported Pennard Golden David (Pennard Golden Sorrel – Pennard Golden Gem) and he became an Irish Ch. in 1953. The Twists also bought and made into Irish Champions Westhyde Rona (Pennard Rusty of Yeo – Westhyde Waxwing), Bryanstown Shannon of Yeo (Ringmaster of Yeo – Bineham Peggy of Yeo), and Bryanstown Camrose Gail (Ch. Camrose Lucius – Camrose Anbria Tamara), and all were

Eng. Ir. Ch. Papeta Philosopher.   *David Dalton.*

good workers as well. When Shannon and Gail were mated they produced English & Ir. Ch. Bryanstown Gail Warning, who also won many Field Trial awards. In 1953 the Twists founded the All Ireland Golden Retriever Club. Their departure to England in 1970 was a great loss to the breed in Ireland, though the Bryanstown Goldens continued with great success in England.

Another important kennel in the south has been the Greenview kennel, owned by Mr and Mrs T. Molany. They made up Ir. Ch. Greenview Abbot (Deerflite Rocket – Daffodil of Oldcastle). They imported Westley Silas of Greenview, one of the outstanding Ch. Westley Victoria – Ch. Nortonwood Faunus litter. He won his Irish title and two CCs and was unlucky not to gain his third CC. Silas has produced many winning progeny. The Tyrol kennel, owned by Mr and Mrs Gaffney, made up Irish Ch. Dabess Paddiwak (Gyrima Todmanton of Dabess – Fern of Dabess), and better still ,English Ch. & Ir. Ch. Papeta Philosopher. He is the sire of Mr and Mrs Bateman's (Compass) Ir. Ch. Isobel of Compass. Another kennel to do well is Maudie Burkes Sandwood kennel.

The Hughes' Windyacres had the big winning Camrose Tara (Ch. Styal Scott of Glengilde – Sh.Ch. Gyrima Wystonia of Camrose), winner of a CC and Reserve CC in England. The Yacanto Kennel showed Ir. Ch. Elzac Antonio of Yacanto and Linchael Wild Orchid at Yacanto.

AUSTRALIA

Australia is a vast area, a continent in its own right, and Goldens can be shown in areas and never compete against or see Goldens from other areas. The breed was first imported from the UK before the Second World war. Early Australian Champions were from Miss Newton-Deakin (of Tone), Mrs Medhurst (Kuldana), Mrs Wills (Arbrook).

In 1954 two imports were to prove very influential: Boltby Comet from Mrs Harrison (Boltby) and Halsham Hazel from Mrs Broomhall (Halsham). Owned by Mr Spencer of New South Wales (Bonspiel), they both became Australian Champions, and when mated together they produced five Champions. When Mr Spencer died Comet and Hazel went to Mr Davis and again produced winners and Champions, but this time under his prefix – Edmay. Mr Philp had bought from Mr Spencer the Australian Champions Bonspiel Goldglint and Goldgleam, and later he bought Aust. Ch. Edmay Day Dawn. All three were sired by Comet out of Hazel, and they founded his influential Kyvalley kennel. For a time the English-bred Benedict of Golconda (bred by Miss Gallop) owned by Mr Edwards was in Australia. Mr Philp mated Aust. Ch. Bonspiel Goldglint to Benedict of Golconda and produced the big-winning Aust. Ch. Kyvalley Kyvar.

In 1961 Mrs Grant of Western Australia (Karadoc) imported English Ch. Iris Of Essendene. She was a lovely bitch, a winner at Field Trials in Great Britain and Australia. Mrs K. Ledingham (Sundials) also had great breeding influence in Western Australia, especially with the Aust. Ch. and worker Storm of Sundials. In 1965 Mr and Mrs Ledingham returned to England. Other imports from the UK that have influenced the breed came from the Yeo, Anbria, Westley, Camrose and Stolford kennels. The dog, Byxfield Lindys Golden Gleam, made his mark. The current breed recordholder in Australia is Ch. Brygolden Oatly Tyron, owned by P. and M. O'Shea with 3500 challenge points (about 105 British Challenge Certificates).

Australia has six Golden Retriever Clubs: The Golden Retriever Club of South Australia, The Golden Retriever Club of Western Australia, The Golden Retriever Club (formed 1964), The Golden Retriever Club of Queensland, The Central Golden Retriever Club Inc New Zealand, and The Golden Retriever Club of Victoria (INC.)

In 1986 I judged in Melbourne for The Golden Retriever Club of Victoria, I really enjoyed the country meeting the people and judging an entry of 250 dogs (still a record, I believe). My Best in Show, Ch. Ferngold Commodore, was sired by a British import, Ch. Glennessa Ingot. My winner had to be good to beat the likes of Ch. Santamaria San Pedro and the lovely, big-winning import, Ch. Channri Cooke. Youngsters on the day, that I admired and who went on to great things, were Ch. Brygolden Oatly Tyrone, Ch. Sundial Sultan and Ch. Tiptree Thousandth Man. First in my puppy class was Buffalo Kingpin, who went on to become a great Champion and in 1988 was Top Golden throughout Australia and New Zealand. My best bitch was Ch. Kingsgold Borna Star, sired by Ch. Carlsden Sansoo Bobby (Ch. Camrose Ohs Buffalo – Sansue Zena). In second place was the great winner Ch. Queenlee Lady Lion, and in third place was Ch. Layanda Josephine, a daughter of Ch. Balandra Delta Darius CDEx. My intermediate bitch winner was another lovely Darius daughter who went on to greater things: this was Ch. Goldog Alpine Serenade, one of the foundation bitches of the Jindabo kennels.

Looking through the 25th Anniversary Year Book of the Golden Retriever Club of Victoria has brought back happy memories of my time in Melbourne. I particularly admired stock from the following kennels: Barbara and John Moores (Tiptrees) and Dual Ch. Tiptree Timothy CD (Ferntip), Pam Collman's very typical Goldog Alpine Goldens, Bert and Phyl Kewish (Tahmero), Derek and Fay Pearson (Jindabo) and Mr and Mrs Sutton with Ch. Channri Cooke. The committee and officers were most helpful, especially Mrs Rose Odell, another breed historian. Judges of their Championship shows are made honorary members of the club, and the regular newsletters keep Golden Retriever enthusiasts in touch.

Aust. Ch. Ferngold Commodore: BIS winner.

Aust. Ch. Goldog Alpine Serenade: A foundation bitch for the Jindabo kennel.

Wayne and Virginia Pearson's Jindabo Limited Edition.

INFLUENTIAL KENNELS
In the last ten years, the following kennels have been active in the show ring:

QUEENLEE: Owned by N. and B. Bolton, this kennel has had many Champions. It was the strongest kennel in the early to mid-1980s; it has started many kennels with foundation stock, and top studs have been at Queenlee for many years. One of the most famous Goldens was the bitch, Ch. Queenlee Lady Lion, who won the CC and BIS at the New South Wales, Victoria, Queensland and South Australian Championship Shows – a feat not repeated by any other dog or bitch. They have owned the famous sire, Ch. & Obedience Ch. Queenlee Debonair, who sired many Champions and Obedience Champions of the eighties.

GOLDTREVE: Owned by F. and B. Hession, this kennel was very active in the early eighties. Their most famous dog was Ch. Goldtreve Cameron, an AI son of Ch. Camrose Cabus Christopher. It can be said Cameron changed the shape of Goldens in Australia and started the move towards the more English type of dog. They imported Ch. Noravon Otto, who produced Ch. Goldtreve Bracken, the influential sire in the later half of the eighties.
GUNARRYN: Owned by Felicity Dyer and Penny Heslop, who campaigned Ch. Goldtreve Bracken and the big-winning bitch of the eighties, Ch. Alubyc Autumn Arwen. This bitch was bred by K. Hollis of Queensland, and she was an All Breeds BIS winner, winning Golden

Mike and Robyn Ramsay's Aust. Ch. Ramgold Rhyme N Reason.

Retriever Club Specialities in NSW and Victoria. Her daughter, Ch. Gunarryn Lady in Red, has also won very well. In the nineties, this kennel has introduced the English lines – Styal, Sansue and Nortonwood – into their own lines.

BUFFALO: This kennel was established in 1970 and owned by Mike and Sandra Patterson. It has consistently produced Champions, including the great Ch. Buffalo Woodbuff CD, and now Ch. Buffalo Kingpin, multi-BIS All Breeds, Speciality and multi-Royal CC winner, and proving a sire of Champions. Aust. NZ Ch. Natinglea Copper Cream went BIS Golden Retriever Club in 1991.

RAMGOLD: Owned by M. and R. Ramsay, this kennel started in 1982 with Ch. Queenlee Nice N Natural as their foundation, who proved a good winner. They imported Aust. Ch Nortonwood Squire in 1984 and Styal Scotts Son of Ramgold CD in 1987, and both dogs have continued the change towards more English style of dogs in Australia. The kennel also boasts Ch. Ramgold Rhyme N Reason, one of the youngest Golden Champions on record to obtained her title, at just eleven months, who had also passed 500 challenge points (about 15 British CCs) by three years old.

KARRELL: This is a very important kennel of many years standing, starting from Ch. Wildheart Caviare CDEx and Ch. Vanrose Karen CD, whose progeny to English Sh.Ch. & NZ Ch. Happy Chance of Stolford made up five Champions. Stolford Sherriff was imported from the UK, and among his influential progeny is the outstanding Ch. Balandra Delta Darius UD. This dog was a prolific winner and his Sydney Royal record of winning Best of Breed three years running, Best Gundog two years running, still stands. In 1981 he went BIS under judge R.M. James at the Sydney Royal from an entry of 5,500. He has gone on to sire many Champions.

LAYANDA: L. and J. Morrison imported from the UK Ch. Folderslane Freewheeler (Sh.Ch. Verdayne Dandini of Davern – Marketsheath Cornflower), who has sired the good-winning bitch Ch. Layanda Fashion & Fame.